INSIGHT

EXF

NEW ENGLAND

⊙ Walking Eye App

Your guide now includes a free eBook to your chosen destination, for the same great price as before. Simply download the Walking Eye App from the App Store or Google Play to access your free eBook.

HOW THE WALKING EYE APP WORKS

Through the Walking Eye App, you can purchase a range of eBooks and destination content. However, when you buy this book, you can download the corresponding eBook for free. Just see below in the grey panel where to find your free content and then scan the QR code at the bottom of this page.

Destinations: Download essential destination content featuring recommended sights and attractions, restaurants, hotels and an A–Z of practical information, all available for purchase.

Ships: Interested in ship reviews? Find independent reviews of river and ocean ships in this section, all available for purchase.

eBooks: You can download your free accompanying digital version of this guide here. You will also find a whole range of other eBooks, all available for purchase.

Free access to travel-related blog articles about different destinations, updated on a daily basis.

HOW THE EBOOKS WORK

The eBooks are provided in EPUB file format. Please note that you will need an eBook reader installed on your device to open the file. Many devices come with this as standard, but you may still need to install one manually from Google Play.

The eBook content is identical to the content in the printed guide.

HOW TO DOWNLOAD THE WALKING EYE APP

1. Download the Walking Eye App from the App Store or Google Play.
2. Open the app and select the scanning function from the main menu.
3. Scan the QR code on this page – you will then be asked a security question to verify ownership of the book.
4. Once this has been verified, you will see your eBook
   in the purchased ebook section, where you will be able to download it.

Other destination apps and eBooks are available for purchase separately or are free with the purchase of the Insight Guide book.

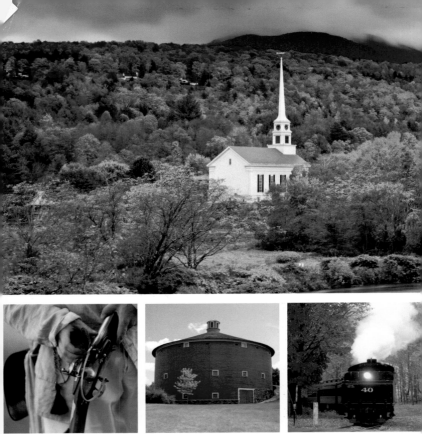

CONTENTS

ACTIVITIES

Climb New England's highest peak, Mount Washington, just one of the many hikes threading the White Mountains (route 13); in winter, head there and to Vermont's Killington (route 10) for skiing.

RECOMMENDED ROUTES FOR...

ARCHITECTURE

Visit Providence (route 7) and Newport (route 8) to see grand civic buildings and the 'cottages' of 19th-century tycoons. For modern architecture see the Frank Gehry-designed Ray and Maria Stata Center at MIT (route 2).

ART FANS

In the Berkshires (route 6), don't miss MASS MoCA and the Norman Rockwell Museum. The Peabody Essex Museum in Salem (route 4) displays an impressive international collection. The art collections of Harvard (route 2), Yale (route 9), and the Rhode Island School of Design (route 7) are all excellent.

CHILDREN

Billings Farm (route 10) and Shelburne Farms (route 11) let kids interact with farmyard animals. New Hampshire's Lakes Region (route 12) and White Mountains (route 13) serve up game arcades, train rides, and theme parks.

FOOD AND DRINK

Boston (route 1) is just one of New England's great culinary destinations; foodies also love Portland (route 15), Portsmouth (route 14), and Cape Cod (route 5), while beer aficionados flock to Vermont's award winning breweries.

HISTORY BUFFS

Acquaint yourself with Colonial and Revolutionary sights on Boston's Freedom Trail (route 1) and between Lexington and Concord (route 3). Journey back in time to the infamous witch trials in Salem on the North Shore.

NATIONAL PARKS

For lush landscapes that burst into autumn colours, Vermont (routes 10 and 11) is justly famous, as are the Berkshires (route 6). Maine's Acadia National Park (route 16) is well worth the trip Down East.

SHOPPERS

The outlet stores of Freeport (route 15) please bargain hunters. Snap up a book or collegiate T-shirt in Harvard (route 2) or Yale (route 9), or Red Sox memorabilia in Boston (route 1).

INTRODUCTION

An introduction to New England's geography, customs, and culture, plus illuminating background information on cuisine, history, and what to do when you're there.

The remote, seaswept coast of Maine

EXPLORE NEW ENGLAND

Six states – Connecticut, Maine, Massachusetts, New Hampshire, Rhode Island, and Vermont – make up New England, a historic playground of sophisticated cities, bucolic villages, seaside resorts, and beautiful countryside.

In the northeast corner of the USA, sandwiched between Canada, New York State, and the Atlantic Ocean, lies New England, home of some of the oldest American archetypes: the white church steeple presiding over a tidy village green, the self-sufficient farmstead, the swimming hole beneath a covered bridge, the salt-sprayed fishing village tucked against a rock-bound coast.

These were just everyday sights for New Englanders until 19th-century Currier & Ives prints and 20th-century Norman Rockwell illustrations introduced them to people who had never set foot in the region. Despite the passage of time, the lush, pastoral visions still exist today and provide a picturesque backdrop for the mixture of walks and driving tours in this guide.

HISTORY

As you travel throughout the region's six states, there is plenty to remind you why it is called New England. Many of the town and city names were adopted from across the Atlantic by 17th-century British settlers. It is here that you find some of America's oldest and most illustrious seats of learning – Harvard, Yale, and Brown – all with campuses modeled on old English universities. Even after political ties with Britain were broken, ideas from the Old World – such as the abolition of slavery and the technology of the Industrial Revolution – found fertile ground here in the 19th century, bringing New England great wealth.

The coming of the railroads also stoked a fledgling tourism industry along the coast and in the mountains, where the wealthy built palatial summer homes and grand hotels. After World War II, tourism in New England became diffused and democratized, especially when entrepreneurs began stringing rope tows, and later, chair lifts, along the sides of mountains that were destined to become ski resorts. National parks and state forests were set up to protect the most precious pieces of the environment for all to enjoy.

CLIMATE

New England has four distinct seasons. The first snow generally falls in November and continues intermittently through March. Spring, (better known as mud season), can be fleeting and is charac-

Vibrant fall colours

terized by crisp, clear days and chilly evenings, often dampened with snow melt. The humidity often turns hot and heavy from June to September, but ocean breezes cool things down along the coast. Fall in New England is glorious, and the bright red, gold, and orange foliage carpeting the rolling hills and mountains in mid-October justly famous.

GETTING AROUND THE STATES

This guide zones in on specially selected key attractions in each state and organizes the suggested itineraries – none lasting more than three days – accordingly. The routes start with walks in Boston and neighboring Cambridge, the most likely access point for the vast majority of visitors. Proceeding in a roughly clockwise direction from Boston, several, if not all, of the routes can be linked up, time permitting, to enable visitors to construct anything from a long weekend in one state to a full month's vacation throughout all of New England. The Points to Note box at the start of each route gives details on how to link with other routes.

Cradle of Liberty

Massachusetts (www.mass.gov), the most populous of the New England sextet, is known as the Cradle of Liberty; it was here that the War of Independence kicked off in 1775. The state continues to live up to its history of liberalism and free thought; this was the first state in the US to legalize same-sex marriages.

There are 183 National Historic Landmarks in Massachusetts. You can view many of these in Boston – the most European of American cities – on day trips to Lexington and Concord (route 3) and out to Salem and Cape Ann (route 4), where the trappings of the wealth that flooded into the region in the subsequent centuries can be assessed.

Going further back, the days of the Pilgrim Fathers can be experienced on a trip down Massachusetts's South Shore and out to the hooked tip of Cape Cod (route 5), dotted with picturesque villages and sweeping ocean vistas. Continue to follow in the footsteps of those earlier adventurers by heading inland to explore Pioneer Valley and the verdant Berkshire Hills (route 6).

The Ocean State

Neighboring Massachusetts to the south is Rhode Island (www.ri.gov). Growing out of the Providence Plantations colony established in 1636 by Roger Williams, a clergyman disillusioned with Massachusetts Bay's theocratic government, the diminutive state was the first of the 13 colonies to cut its ties with Britain.

Rhode Islanders are seldom more than 30 minutes' drive from the water in the Ocean State. Riverside Providence (route 7), the state capital, has recently emerged from the shadow of Boston as one of New England's most interesting and design-driven cities. Down the coast, chichi Newport (route 8) continues to be a summer haven for the rich, although these days,

Covered bridge in Vermont

for the price of admission, anyone is free to traipse through the town's jaw-dropping collection of 19th-century mansions.

The Constitution State

Taking its name from a Mohegan (a Native American tribe) word meaning 'place of the long tidal river', Connecticut's proximity to New York often means it gets overlooked as a part of New England.

The state is bisected by the mighty Connecticut River, while its south edge raggedly borders the Long Island Sound. Along the latter you will find the kitsch maritime shops of Mystic, the naval base of New London, and the academic haunts of New Haven (route 9).

Mountains and forests

It is in the next two states that the natural beauty of New England really starts to come to the fore. Sparsely populated Vermont (www.vermont.gov) may be landlocked, but it is notable for vast Lake Champlain, running down half of the state's west border. Overlooking the lake is Vermont's largest city, Burlington (route 11), one of the most laid-back of New England's urban centers. To get there, you pass through the lush Green Mountains (route 10), starting in the arty town of Brattleboro and heading towards peaks that are home to some of New England's top ski resorts.

The modern history of New Hampshire (www.nh.gov) is almost as old as that of Massachusetts, with the first English settlements in Portsmouth (route 14) dating back to 1623. You will begin to understand why it is known as the Granite State when you head inland to tour the magnificent White Mountains (route 13), rugged peaks that rise up over 3,000ft (915m). At the foot of the mountains lies the equally majestic Lakes Region (route 12).

North by Down East

Last, but by no means least, there is Maine (www.maine.gov), the largest of the New England states. Many visitors barely scratch the surface of what the Pine Tree State has to offer, sticking mainly to the 60-mile (96km) stretch of coast south of Portland. Here the towns of York, Ogunquit, Wells, and Kennebunkport all enjoy fine beaches.

But it is north of Portland (route 15) that Maine's character asserts itself most clearly, along the ragged coastline to the far-flung Down East redoubts of Bar Harbor and Acadia National Park (route 16). With more time on your hands, you could really go off the beaten track to some of the unspoiled islands that flake off from the shoreline like thousands of rocky, pine-tree-clad crumbs.

POPULATION

Around 14.44 million people live in New England, about three quarters of them based in and around the biggest cities, such as Boston, Providence, and Hartford, in the southern states of Massachusetts, Rhode Island, and Connecticut, respectively. This leaves much of the rest

Burlington's waterfront

Federal-style architecture in Massachusetts

of the region with a low population density and a traditional rural character and attitude, in sharp contrast to the more multicultural urban centers toward the coast.

Nearly 15 million people call New England home. Over 22 percent of them are under the age of 18; 13 percent are over 65. Of these, the majority are Cauca-

DON'T LEAVE NEW ENGLAND WITHOUT...

Indulging in 'chowda'. New England long Atlantic coastline provides lots of fresh fish and seafood, especially clams, which overflow the creamy rich chowder the region is famous for. Go all the way and order it served in a bread bowl. See page 17.

Watching the whales. Humpback, finback, right, and minke whales enjoy the rich feeding grounds of New England, making it a prime spot for beholding their aquatic majesty on watching tours, particularly from Cape Cod. See page 22.

Peeping the leaves. New England unveils its true colors every autumn in an astonishing glow of reds, golds, and oranges, particularly in the heavily forested areas of northern New England. See page 74.

Walking the Marginal Way in Ogunquit. Seventeen miles (27km) up the coast from Portsmouth (see page 88), New England's most dramatic and romantic seaside promenade stretches 1.25 miles (2km) along the bluffs, coves, and inlets of Ogunquit. Crashing waves included.

Rooting for the Red Sox at Fenway Park. Whether you support Boston's love-em-or-hate-em team, a trip to century-old Fenway Park is a step back to the glory days of baseball and a glimpse of New England's beating heart. See page 22.

Exploring the mansions of Newport. The aristocracy of the guilded age endowed Newport, Rhode Island with some of the finest manors in the country, most of which are open for tours and vicarious dreams. See page 68.

Taking to the slopes. The mountains of New England, particularly in Vermont and New Hampshire, are home to some of the country's best skiing. All levels are welcomed and catered to. Off-season, hikers replace ski bums on the trails and peaks. See page 23.

Cycling the Burlington Bike Path. Along Lake Champlain, the 'west coast' of New England, one of the region's best bike paths runs 14 miles (22.5km) from Burlington to the Islands. Bikes are available on site to rent. See page 74.

Sip suds at craft breweries. Since Boston's own Samuel Adams launched the craft brew revolution in 1985, New England has remained at the sudsy edge of beer production. Indeed, Vermont has the most breweries per capita in the country. See page 19.

Time travel to Days of Yore. New England's maritime and pilgrim past are kept alive at period parks throughout the region, most notably at Mystic Seaport in Connecticut and Plimoth Plantation in Massachusetts. See page 72.

sian (83 percent), far outnumbering the next largest groups – Hispanic, African-American, and Asian-American. Massa-chusetts has the largest population, with over 6.5 million residents; Vermont has only 625,000.

Of the European-originated population, English dominance has been superseded by those of Irish, French/French Canadian, and Italian descent. The centers of population break down along ethnic lines. Boston has a large Irish and Italian population which is more numerous now than those who trace their lineage to the city's British roots. Rhode Island has strong Italian connections, but Providence boasts a large Portuguese neighborhood. Northern Vermont and New Hampshire have a strong French influence due to proximity to Quebec.

A literary tradition

One the best ways to gain an insight into the New England frame of mind is to read a book by one of its native writers. In the 19th century, authors centered in Boston and Concord created the first important movement in American literature. In 1836 Ralph Waldo Emerson published his philosophical essay *Nature*, while in the following years Emerson's neighbor, Henry David Thoreau, chronicled his relationship with the natural world and his sojourn in a hand-built cabin on the shores of Walden Pond (see page 49).

Nathaniel Hawthorne brought a psychological aspect to the American novel, casting a sharp eye on Puritan New England in *The Scarlet Letter* (1850); his friend Herman Melville used his knowledge of New Bedford's whaling industry as background for *Moby-Dick* (1851).

Adding further luster to New England's literary reputation in the mid-19th century were Louisa May Alcott (also a Concord resident), Henry Wadsworth Longfellow (whose home is preserved in Harvard, see page 44), and Mark Twain, who settled in Hartford, Connecticut. Toward the end of the 19th-century, the Pulitzer Prize-winning author Edith Wharton took up residence in a grand house in Lenox (see page 64).

POLITICS, RELIGION AND ECONOMICS

Long known for its liberalism, New England is the heartland of the Democratic Party. However, three of the region's states (Vermont, Maine, and Massachusetts) have Republican governors.

Spiritually, the original Pilgrims would be displeased, at best, by the region's religious affiliations. Given the influx of Irish, Italian, Portuguese, and Hispanic immigrants, it's no surprise that 36 percent of New Englanders are Catholic, with another 32 percent identifying themselves as Christian. But 25 percent claim no religious affiliation of any kind, one of the highest levels in the country, perhaps in keeping with the region's liberal politics.

Boston's skyline as viewed across the Inner Harbour

As in the past, New England's prime industries revolve around specialized foods (lobsters, chowder, cranberries, and maple syrup) and manufacturing, particularly electronic equipment. While this last sector took a hit during the last economic downturn, the region's tourism industry remains buoyant.

TOP TIPS FOR VISITING NEW ENGLAND

Before you go. For more travel information on New England, go to www.visitnewengland.com, or check out the tourism websites of each of the states.

Dress in layers. The weather of New England changes often, ranging from wet, hot humidity in the summer to frigid cold in the winter, and everything in between. Dressing in layers allows greater adaptation.

Invest in footwear. Even if there's not several feet of snow on the ground in the winter, or an almost equal amount of mud in spring, New England's rugged countryside means tough, quality footwear is essential.

Carry bug spray. Outside of Boston, much of New England is wet and rural. That means any walk in the woods can quickly turn to torture without mosquito repellent. Also check yourself and pets for ticks.

Book early for fall. October is peak foliage and tourist season in New England, making accommodation very hard to find if not booked up to six months in advance.

Bring a car. The only city with a major public transport system in New England is Boston. A few railways do connect all six states, but without a car, exploration is a challenge.

Go off-highway. Well-maintained highways offer fast, easy routes through the states, but far more vintage charm lies along the old routes, which snake along rivers and valleys through Colonial towns and villages, albeit at a much slower pace.

Eat and drink locally. Although it's easy to find major restaurant chains, the region prides itself on fresh, locally sourced meals, which are never far away, along with some of the world's best breweries.

Refresh your history. New England, particularly the Boston area, is replete with major historical sights pertaining to the founding of the United States, from Plymouth Rock to Bunker Hill. This is the place to bring those history lessons to life.

Catch a bus. On Saturday and Sunday from mid-April to early May and then daily until mid-October, the Liberty Ride (tel: 781-862-0500; www.libertyride.us) tour bus travels between Lexington and Concord visiting the key historic sites. It's a 90-minute continuous loop guided tour, and you can hop on and off as you please within a 48-hour period.

Stay off the Cape on summer holidays. Cape Cod is indeed a beauty, but torturous to reach around any major holiday in the summer, when the one major road, Route 6, grinds almost to a halt with traffic.

Pack paper maps. Although cellphone coverage remains strong around urban centers, more rural areas, particularly mountainous ones, can severely weaken, and even kill, signals. So be sure to bring back-up.

Fresh lobster

FOOD AND DRINK

While proudly aware of its traditionalist roots, New England cuisine looks firmly to the future. In the region's top kitchens, some of America's best chefs make use of the top-grade local produce to tune up old favorites and invent new ones.

The culinary tradition of New England synthesizes old English cookery techniques with the ingredients that were available to the colonies. A dish such as New England boiled dinner – beef brisket poached with root vegetables and cabbage – might easily have graced an English table 300 years ago. In terms of local additions, early New Englanders could dip into an immense natural larder bursting with game, fish and shellfish, native berries, and that great gift of the Native Americans, corn (maize).

The first Thanksgiving was celebrated in Plymouth in 1621 by the 50 or so *Mayflower* Pilgrims who had survived the initial year in New England. It has since become the US's major holiday tradition, complete with turkey, cranberries, and corn – all staple New England ingredients.

TRADITIONAL STANDBYS

Today's visitors to the region will have no trouble finding old standbys, such as Yankee pot roast (similar to the boiled dinner, but made with prime roast beef and a thickened gravy), creamy clam or fish chowder, and Indian pudding. The latter, a baked corn porridge affair, is usually served – as it definitely wasn't during colonial times – with vanilla ice cream. But these time-honored dishes have largely been relegated to the menus of restaurants that make a specialty of them, and of 'ye olde' colonial decor, too.

That said, the local, organic, small-batch movement has taken firm hold of New England, with chefs taking full advantage of the immense natural resources locally to produce a new generation of regional dishes that link the

Boston Baked Beans for sale

Preparations at Boston's Union Oyster House

present to the past, and the region to the world. Even many international restaurants have hopped on board, filling tortillas, empanadas, and vegetable rolls with local produce, dairy, and meat, particularly in cities and college towns, which offer a broad range of world cuisines – none more so than Boston.

Back in the 18th century, the city of Boston was awash with molasses shipped in from the Caribbean as part of the rum trade. This was mixed with salt pork and beans to make baked beans, once the quintessential Boston dish – hence the city's nickname, Beantown. These days, baked beans are not a common menu item; if you fancy trying them head to Union Oyster House (see page 39).

ETHNIC AND TRENDY

The diverse immigrant population of New England's principal city, Boston, has bequeathed it a fine range of ethnic restaurants. Chinatown is primarily packed with – you guessed it – Chinese restaurants, but it also has a smattering of Malaysian, Vietnamese, and Japanese eateries, too.

The North End's vibe is almost exclusively Italian, from simple red-and-white-tablecloth cafés to sleek temples to regional cuisine. For the trendiest dining spots, the South End and its SoWa (South of Washington) district are the places to head – between Tremont Street and Harrison Avenue you will never go hungry.

Seafood, naturally, is a big feature of the Waterfront and up-and-coming Fort Point Channel areas, while the academic areas around Harvard and MIT are prime hunting grounds for good-value, atmospherically vibrant and cosmopolitan restaurants and cafés. Cambridge's reputation for healthy organic cooking is deserved, but the town is also no slouch at fine dining. When it comes to discovering hot new chefs, it is this side of the Charles River that often proves the more fertile.

ABUNDANT SEAFOOD

New England's seafood tradition is not to be confused with that of other American coastal regions, such as Louisiana or the Pacific Northwest. Fried clams, for instance, are never better than those found along the North Shore of Massachusetts.

A drive along the Maine coast can become a movable feast of lobster; you can have it boiled and served roadside 'in the rough,' cubed or shredded with lashings of mayonnaise or melted butter in bulging rolls, or in rich bisques and stews. Wellfleet oysters, Chatham scallops from Cape Cod, and freshly caught swordfish and bluefish are all considered to be among the world's greatest saltwater treats.

You should not miss out on trying authentic chowder packed with clams. You will also come across 'steamers,' soft-shelled clams so called because

Modern Diner, a 1941 Sterling Streamliner, in Rhode Island

they are steam-cooked. Hard-shell clams come in several varieties, such as littlenecks, cherrystones, and quahogs. In many of New England's coastal cities, raw bars offer the chance to eat them au natural.

The term 'scrod' is used for white-fleshed fish. One story has it that the word sprung from the acronym for Select Catch Remains On Deck, the appellation sea captains would give to the best batches of fish.

CULINARY SPECIALTIES

When it comes to culinary curiosities, New England certainly has its share. All of the following can be found in the region: French Canadian-style breakfasts, with baked beans crowding eggs and sausages; clam pizza in Connecticut; vinegar-marinated Portuguese pork and seafood dishes that are especially common in southeastern Massachusetts; and muffins (or pancakes) packed with blueberries, which can frequently be purchased from roadside outlets in Maine.

Dairy specialties

The milk from the many cows you will spot grazing pastures in Vermont is used to produce some of the region's best cheese. Cabot (www.cabotcheese.coop) is the biggest producer of Vermont cheddar, but they've been joined by dozens of small-batch cheese makers, most notably in Grafton; you will find a wide selection of these products at Quechee Gorge Village near Woodstock. You should also sample the quality dairy products of Shelburne Farms. The milk is not just used for cheese; Ben Cohen and Jerry Greenfield started making their now-famous crazy-flavoured ice creams in Vermont in 1978; drop by their factory in Waterbury (www.benjerry.com) for a tour.

WHERE TO EAT

New England has its fair share of fancy restaurants, ranging from the paneled elegance of old-school places such as Boston's Parker's Restaurant (where JFK proposed to Jackie; see page 109) or Nick's in Providence to the more relaxed, cutting-edge operations of Portland, Maine, Portsmouth, New Hampshire, and Burlington, Vermont.

If you are after a quick, cheap bite, you can hardly do better – or have a more authentic American dining experience – than at a diner. The diner phenomenon was born in Providence, Rhode Island, and matured in Worcester, Massachusetts, where the Worcester Lunch Car Company churned out

Food and drink prices

Throughout this guide, the average price for a three-course dinner for one, excluding beverages, tax, and tip:
$$$$ = over $60
$$$ = $40–60
$$ = $20–40
$ = below $20

Boston's top ale

Dining at the Top of the Hub, Boston

over 600 pre-fabricated diner units up until the early 1960s. They are great places for breakfast; for one incorporating choice local products, head to Chelsea Royal Diner in West Brattleboro. Just down the road, T. J. Buckley's brings it full circle by using a handsomely renovated 1927 diner as a base for its fine-dining experience.

WHAT TO DRINK

When it comes to soft drinks, perhaps the one most associated with New England is cranberry juice; drive along Cape Cod to view the many cranberry bogs from which the luscious crimson berries are harvested each fall. There is even a cranberry festival held each year in Carver, Massachusetts (www.edaville.com). Spiked with vodka, the juice becomes a cocktail known as a Cape Codder.

Cafés and coffee milk

Café culture is alive and healthy throughout New England – in the college towns in particular you will seldom have to search far for a quirky, characterful joint in which to sip your morning brew, rather than an identikit Starbucks. While in Rhode Island, though, those with a sweet tooth might want to sample coffee milk, a mix of milk and syrupy condensed black coffee. The drink caught on after Italian immigrants introduced it to locals in the 1920s. It has become so popular that it was declared the state's official drink in 1993.

Beers and microbrews

Founding father Samuel Adams was a brew master, so it is natural that one of Boston's principal breweries should have adopted his name. It started as a micro-brewery in 1985; you will now find Sam Adams ales and lagers (www.samueladams.com) in bars across the region. The other Boston beermaker that has hit the big time is Harpoon (www.harpoonbrewery.com); drop by their brewery for tours, tastings, and beery events on holidays.

Boston microbreweries that have stayed micro include Boston Beer Works (www.beerworks.net), with branches near Fenway Park and the North End, and Cambridge Brewing Company (www.cambrew.com) near MIT. Vermont has become particularly famous for its thriving microbrewery industry, with many of the best rated breweries in the world; join Burlington Brew Tours (tel: 802-760-609; www.burlingtonbrewtours.com) for a tour of several Lake Champlain area breweries.

Wine

You may be surprised to discover that New England has a small wine industry. From Newport in Rhode Island, you can follow the Coastal Wine Trail of southeastern New England (www.coastalwinetrail.com), taking in 14 wineries. Connecticut also promotes a wine trail (www.ctwine.com), covering 24 of the state's vineyards, and while in Maine, you might want to sample the wines flavored with local blueberries and other fruits.

Traditional candlemaking at Yankee Candle

SHOPPING

From enormous malls packed with famous labels to dusty antiques shops and cozy craft-stores, New England offers a wealth of shopping opportunities.

Most stores open Monday to Saturday 9am to 7pm, and shopping malls generally stay open until 9pm. On Sunday opening hours are typically noon to 5pm or 6pm. Many smaller, independently owned shops are closed on Sunday.

BOSTON SHOPS

For the most comprehensive range of shopping, the region's biggest city, Boston, can't be beaten. Back Bay, with its Newbury Street couturiers and upscale Prudential Center and Copley Place shops (Louis Vuitton, Hugo Boss, and Michael Kors) is the main area to hit, while Downtown there's Faneuil Hall Marketplace, featuring dozens of specialty shops in restored historic buildings.

ANTIQUES

Having been settled for nearly 400 years, New England was the first part of the country to realize that a fortune was hidden in its attics and basements. In Boston, antique dealers are clustered along Charles Street in Beacon Hill. Specialties of the district include high-end furniture, porcelain and silver, and marine paint-

ings (although most of the city's most respected antique-art dealers are on Newbury Street in Back Bay).

Outside the city, eastern Massachusetts's biggest concentration of dealers is in the North Shore town of Essex, where more than a dozen shops specialize in fine English furniture and 18th-century New England pieces. Out on Cape Cod, in Provincetown, dealers tend to favor kitsch items from the mid-20th century. Several times each year, the western Massachusetts town of Brimfield hosts New England's biggest antiques event (www.brimfieldshow.com). Hundreds of dealers converge to trade.

Between Burlington and Shelburne, Route 7 in Vermont has a fine concentration of antique shops, or try Putnam, New Preston, Woodbury, and Old Saybrook in Connecticut.

ARTS AND CRAFTS

New England's tradition of fine craftsmanship dates back to colonial times, when things were handmade by necessity. For beautiful examples of this type of work, head to the Hancock Shaker Village, where excellent modern reproduc-

Faneuil Hall Marketplace   *Red Sox fans*

tions of the religious sect's cherrywood boxes, handmade brooms, functional furniture, and other crafts are for sale.

The region continues to attract and inspire artisans who want to live and work in a place where they can absorb inspiration from the past and find a ready market among quality-conscious locals and visitors. The League of New Hampshire Craftsmen is an association of Granite State artisans – potters, jewelers, woodworkers, glass blowers, and weavers – who sell their work at eight state locations, including the league's place of origin, Center Sandwich Fine Craft Gallery. In summer, many Vermont artists bring their wares, and even workshops, to the sprawling weekend Farmers' Market, which covers City Hall Park and surrounding streets. Similar markets can be found in Portland, Concord, and Norfolk.

Fine glassware is associated with Sandwich on Cape Cod. You can watch glass being hand-blown by Pairpoint Glass (www.pairpoint.com) in nearby Sagamore, which lays claim to being America's oldest glassworks.

Portland, Maine, has a reputation for its art scene. You can browse many commercial galleries in and around the city's Old Port District, where you will also find fine local pottery at the Maine Potters Market (www.mainepottersmarket.com).

SPECIALTY SHOPPING

Some New England specialty stores have become destinations in them-

selves. Orvis (www.orvis.com) in Manchester, Vermont, has a country-chic persona built around its handmade fly rods and fishing tackle. In Maine, Kittery Trading Post (www.kitterytradingpost.com) will outfit a country expedition with nearly as much panache as at L.L. Bean (see box). Peter Limmer and Sons (www.limmercustomboot.com) in Intervale, New Hampshire, make fine hiking boots.

And if you can't find a special item anywhere else, be sure to try Vermont Country Store in Weston.

Outlet shopping

New England's factory-outlet phenomenon has two points of origin. One was the availability of inexpensive floor space in once-thriving mill towns, such as Fall River, Massachusetts. The other factor was the success of outdoor equipment and clothing supplier L.L. Bean; its 24-hour-a-day store in Freeport, Maine, drew so many visitors that other retailers moved in for a share of the market. Today, scores of top-name purveyors of men's and women's clothing, housewares, and gifts have set up shop in downtown Freeport, where you can find bargains on overstock, last-season, and second-quality items. The formula has been adopted in North Conway, New Hampshire; Manchester, Vermont; Kittery, Maine; Wrentham and Lee, Massachusetts; and Clinton, Connecticut.

Sailing on the Charles in Boston

OUTDOOR ACTIVITIES

New Englanders are passionate about sports, with baseball and football the most enthusiastically supported. The region's great outdoors also provides a stage for a range of adventurous activities, from whale-watching to snowboarding.

SPECTATOR SPORTS

Generally, when it comes to watching top-league spectator sport in New England, you are going to be heading to Boston, for baseball, football, and basketball.

Whale-watching

The humpbackgathering at the fertile feeding-ground Stellwagen Bank, 25 miles (40km) off the Boston coast, is one of the greatest in the world. Minkie whales can be seen too. Boston Harbor Cruises (tel: 617-227-4321; www.bostonharborcruises.com) run whale-watching tours in conjunction with New England Aquarium from Boston's Long and Central wharves respectively.

The season runs from April to October, with the peak around June. Cruises take around three hours, and commentary is provided by naturalists. The water can be rough, so it is worth carrying anti-sea-sickness tablets. Rainwear is useful in April and May, and you should dress warmly even in summer. Whale-watching tours also depart from Gloucester, Plymouth, and Provincetown.

Baseball

In 2004 the city's Major League base-ball team finally broke the losing 'curse' in the World Series championships that had haunted them for 86 years – ever since the legendary slugger Babe Ruth was sold to eternal rivals, the New York Yankees. To prove their new-found form, the Red Sox (www.redsox.com) snatched more World Series victories in 2007 and 2013, much to the delight of Bostonians who turned out en masse to welcome their heroes home with ticker-tape parades.

Football

The Red Sox can now proudly stand shoulder to shoulder with the city's American football team, the New England Patriots (www.patriots.com). Five-time winners of the Super Bowl, all since 2002, the Patriots are loved with a particular fervor nowadays. Their home ground is the Gillette Stadium at Foxborough, 32 miles (51.5km) south of Boston, and the season runs from late August to late December. Also playing at the Gillette Stadium is the professional soccer team New England Revolution (www.revolutionsoccer.net).

Rafting in the Berkshires   *Hiking the Appalachian Trail*

Ice hockey and basketball
From October to mid-April in T.D. Garden stadium, above Boston's North Station, you can catch games either by the city's ice-hockey team, the Bruins (www.boston bruins.com), or the basketball team, the Celtics (www.nba.com/celtics).

For all the hoopla over the Red Sox, Patriots, or Bruins, it is the Celtics who are the most successful Boston team in any major sport in the country. Beginning in 1959, they won an unprecedented eight National Basketball Association (NBA) championships in a row, and to date, have 17 NBA titles to their credit, the most recent in 2008.

Boston Marathon
With over 30,000 runners, including Olympic champions, the Boston Marathon (www.baa.org) is the world's oldest annually contested long-distance running race, the first one taking place back in 1867. It is the most-watched sporting event in New England, with about 500,000 spectators annually.

OUTDOOR ACTIVITIES

New England is a dream destination for those who desire an activity-driven vacation. Miles of coastlines and islands, not to mention multiple rivers and lakes, mean that sailing, canoeing, kayaking, and white-water rafting are all possibilities. The oceans also provide a venue for one of the most thrilling of wildlife displays – sightings of whales (see box).

Fly- and deep-sea fishing are also popular pursuits.

The mountains and forests of Maine, Massachusetts, New Hampshire, and Vermont are the perfect settings for winter skiing vacations; head to mega resorts, such as Bretton Woods, Loon, Killington, Jay Peak, and Stowe, home of the Trapp Family Lodge (www.trappfamily.com) of *The Sound of Music* fame. Come summer, the same locations are ideal for hiking and mountain biking, not to mention cool dips in swimming holes.

Hiking and climbing
In New Hampshire's Franconia Notch State Park, you can tackle an 8-mile (13km) section of the 2,175-mile (3,500km) long Appalachian Trail (www.nps.gov/appa), which runs across all the New England states bar Rhode Island. To find out more about this, the first National Scenic Trail, contact the Appalachian Trail Conservancy (www.appalachiantrail.org).

North Conway is a center for outdoor pursuits in New Hampshire; here you will find the International Mountain Climbing School (www.ime-usa.com), as well as the Eastern Mountain Sports Climbing School (www.emsoutdoors.com).

Not to be missed is spectacular Acadia National Park, the only such park in New England, threaded through with 115 miles (185km) of hiking trails. Equally impressive are the dunes and beaches of the Cape Cod National Seashore, covering the entire eastern shoreline of the Outer Cape.

Boston Symphony Orchestra

ENTERTAINMENT

*Serious music, dance, and theater performances take place throughout
New England. There is also a lively popular music scene with many
small clubs and venues, and a packed summer schedule of arts festivals.*

BOSTON

Given Boston's reputation as a bastion of high culture, and the presence of so many institutions of higher learning, including the respected Berklee College of Music, it is no wonder that the city is blessed with a vibrant performing-arts scene and a diverse range of entertainment venues. Pick up a free copy of *The Improper Bostonian* (www.improper. com) or check out DigBoston (http://dig boston.com) to see who and what is playing around Boston, and the lowdown on the hottest clubs.

The BosTix booths beside Faneuil Hall (Tue–Sun 10am–4pm; ww.bostix. org) and on the corner of Copley Square (Thu–Fri 11am–5pm, Sat–Sun 10am–4pm) sell half-price tickets for many events (cash only) on performance day.

Classical music, opera, and dance
For classical music, review the concert schedule for the beautiful Symphony Hall, which hosts the world-class Boston Symphony Orchestra (BSO; www.bso. org), founded in 1881, from November to May. The orchestra can occasionally be heard outdoors at the Hatch Shell in the Esplanade beside the Charles River, where you may also catch the BSO's spin-off Boston Pops Orchestra.

Another excellent venue is Jordan Hall at the New England Conservatory of Music, which stages many free concerts, alongside ones by established ensembles such as the Boston Philharmonic (tel: 617-236-0999; www.bostonphil.org).

Opera, not Boston's strong point, is covered by the Boston Lyric Opera (tel: 617-542-4912; www.blo.org). However, the Boston Ballet (tel: 617-695-6955; www.bostonballet.org) is one of the top dance companies in the US.

Rock and pop
The stars of the music world regularly turn up at the city's biggest venues, such as the outdoor Blue Hills Bank Pavilion (www.bostonpavilion.net; May–September only) out on South Boston Waterfront, and T.D. Garden (www.tdgarden.com), or medium-sized spaces such as the shabby-chic Orpheum Theatre (tel: 617-482-0106; www.orpheum-theater.com).

However, with all those students around, there is an enormous range of small live-music venues and a thriving indie-rock scene of bands and singers to

Tanglewood Music Festival

fill them. Check out places such as the Middle East, The Sinclair, Great Scott, and Paradise Rock Club (see page 119).

Theater

Boston has a small but lively theater scene, with the city's grandest theaters such as the Wang and the Shubert (both part of the Boch Center; see page 118) often used for tryouts of Broadway-bound productions. The city's equivalent of *The Mousetrap* is the comic whodunit *Shear Madness*, staged since 1980 at the Charles Playhouse. For theater and ticket information, see www.boston-theater.com.

The most reliable places for interesting productions are The American Repertory Theatre (tel: 617-547-8300; www.amrep.org) over in Harvard, the Huntington (tel: 617-266-0800; www.huntingtontheatre.org) and the Boston Center for the Arts (tel: 617-426-5000; www.bcaonline.org), with four stages.

OUTSIDE BOSTON

New Haven, home to Yale University, also has a prestigious arts scene, with its New Haven Symphony Orchestra (tel: 203-865-0831; www.newhavensymphony.org) and several theaters, including Yale Repertory Theatre (see page 120), where you can catch budding stars from the Yale School of Drama.

Elsewhere, the region's top cultural offerings tend to cluster in college towns and large cities. Connecticut's Hartford Symphony (tel: 860-987-5900; www.hartfordsymphony.org), Maine's Portland Symphony Orchestra (tel: 207-773-6128; www.portlandsymphony.com), the Vermont Symphony Orchestra (tel: 802-864-5741; www.vso.org), and the Rhode Island Philharmonic (tel: 401-248-7000; www.ri-philharmonic.org) perform at home and throughout their respective states.

Summer arts festivals

There are several major arts festivals held each summer in the Berkshires, which are well worth planning your trip around. The Jacob's Pillow Dance Festival (tel: 413-243-0745; www.jacobspillow.org) held in Becket, 10 miles (16km) east of Lee, runs from June to August. Ballet, modern, and folk troupes perform on indoor and outdoor stages.

A mile out of central Lenox (see page 64) is the 400-acre (160ha) Tanglewood estate (297 West Street; tel: 617-266-1492). Since 1934 this has been the summer home of the Boston Symphony Orchestra. From late June to early September, the prestigious Tanglewood Music Festival (www.bso.org) is held here, ranging from classical to jazz and blues. Pack a picnic and arrive a few hours before a performance to enjoy the magical atmosphere. Also in summer, Lenox hosts the Shakespeare & Co. Drama Festival (tel: 413-637-3353; www.shakespeare.org), including some free events.

Settlers mingle with Native Americans at Plimoth Plantation

HISTORY: KEY DATES

The region has been shaped by the blending and clashing of old England traditions and New World values, from the arrival of the Pilgrims in 1620, through the Salem witch trials and the Revolution, to today's mass tourism.

PRE-REVOLUTIONARY NEW ENGLAND

1602	English explorer Captain Bartholomew Gosnold sights Cape Cod.
1614	Captain John Smith voyages down the coasts of Maine and Massachusetts and dubs the area New England.
1620	The *Mayflower* Pilgrims arrive at Plymouth.
1623	The first English settlements are established in New Hampshire.
1633–6	The first English settlements are set up in Connecticut.
1636	Harvard College, the nation's first institution of higher learning, is founded at Cambridge, Massachusetts. Religious dissident Roger Williams founds the Rhode Island colony.
1692	Twenty people are executed for witchcraft at Salem.
1704	French and allied Native Americans stage the Deerfield Raid, killing many settlers and taking captives to Canada.
1754–63	The French and Indian War, with New England fighting on the British side, ends France's American empire.
1765	The Stamp Act tax stirs anti-British feeling.

THE BATTLE FOR INDEPENDENCE

1770	British soldiers fire on a mob, killing five, in 'Boston Massacre.'
1775	The American Revolution begins with the battles of Lexington and Concord. The Battle of Bunker Hill follows in June.
1776	The British are driven from Boston.
1783	The American Revolution ends.
1791	Vermont becomes the 14th state.

19TH CENTURY

1812–14	War with Britain.

Battle of Lexington in 1775

1820	Maine, once part of Massachusetts, becomes a separate state.
1822	The Merrimack Manufacturing Company is founded at Lowell, Massachusetts, harbinger of the region's industrial prowess.
1830–6	The first New England railroads link Boston with outlying cities.
1845–50	Thousands flee Ireland's potato famine and settle in Boston.
1861–5	Staunchly abolitionist New England sends troops to fight in the Civil War.

20TH CENTURY

c.1900	Amoskeag Mills in Manchester, New Hampshire, constitute the largest textile producer in the world.
1934	The advent of the first mechanical ski tow in Vermont; huge regional industry develops after World War II.
1935	Amoskeag Mills close, as the textile industry moves south.
1960	Bostonian John F. Kennedy is elected president
1960s	High-tech industry booms along Massachusetts's Route 128.
1990s	Limitations are imposed on cod fishing in response to dwindling stocks; numerous traditional livelihoods are threatened.
1999	Vermont adopts 'civil unions'; five years later Massachusetts becomes the first state to legalize same-sex marriage.

21ST CENTURY

2003	New Hampshire's iconic rock formation known as the Old Man of the Mountain collapses despite several efforts to secure it.
2004	The Boston Red Sox break an 87-year losing streak by winning the World Series. Harvard students set up Facebook.
2009	New Hampshire becomes the sixth US state to allow same-sex marriage, bringing it into line with Connecticut, Maine, Massachusetts, and Vermont.
2013	During the Boston Marathon two bombs explode near the finish line, killing 3 people and injuring 264
2014	Vermont House passes the first law in the country to require the labeling of genetically modified food
2017	The governors of four New England states vow to uphold the goals of the Paris Climate Agreement, following President Donald Trump's decision to take the US out of it.

BEST ROUTES

Just across Charles Street from the common is the glorious Public Garden

BOSTON

The Freedom Trail, running from Boston Common to Charlestown, is lined with notable sites that recall the city's Revolutionary history. En route, the North End, Boston's Little Italy, is a great place to eat and drink.

DISTANCE: 5.5 miles (8.75km)
TIME: A full day
START: Boylston T Station
END: Community College T Station
POINTS TO NOTE: Downtown is busy with office workers Monday to Friday, particularly around lunchtime, so a good time to start this walk is mid-morning after rush hour or at the weekend. On Friday and Saturday there is also a lively fresh produce market near Haymarket T Station. The North End is a good area to return to in the evening for dinner. Boston's main Visitor Information Booth (tel: 617-536-4100; www.bostonusa. com; Mon–Fri 8.30am–5pm, Sat–Sun 9am–5pm) is located on the northeast edge of Boston Common just south of the Park Street T Station. You can pick up free maps here or book a place on one of the daily tours offered by the Freedom Trail Foundation (tel: 617-357-8300; www.thefreedomtrail.org), which begin from here.

Capital of Massachusetts, Boston likes to think of itself as the 'Cradle of Liberty' or the 'Hub of the Universe,' a city where modern America started and found its distinctive, independent voice. This route, which shadows the Freedom Trail, features significant landmarks that figured in the decisive break that New England's settlers made from the British in 1776. Established in 1958 to preserve these key monuments and sights, the trail is marked by a red-brick or painted line on the pavement.

BOSTON COMMON AND DOWNTOWN

From Boylston T Station, walk to **Boston Common ❶**, established in 1634 and the oldest public park in the US. Originally used as a 'Comon Field' *(sic)* on which sheep and cattle grazed (they did so up until 1830), the pentagonal space, covering about 50 acres (20ha), was also used as a mustering ground for militias and a venue for public hangings. Within the common, you will find the **Central Burying Ground ❷** (daily dawn–dusk),

Ornate ceiling in the Massachusetts State House

the city's fourth-oldest cemetery; the 70ft (21m) **Soldiers and Sailors Monument ❸**, dedicated to the Union forces killed in the Civil War; and **Frog Pond ❹**, used as a children's wading pool in summer and an ice rink in winter.

At the crest of Beacon Street, on the northwest edge of Boston Common, is the Massachusetts State House (tel: 617-727-3676; www.sec.state.ma.us; guided tours Mon–Fri 10am–3.30pm; free), designed by preeminent city architect Charles Bulfinch and completed in 1798. This regal building's most visually impressive feature, the glittering dome crowned in gold leaf in 1861, was originally covered with shingles.

Park Street

On the corner of Park and Tremont streets stands **Park Street Church ❺** (tel: 617-523-3383; www.parkstreet.org; mid-June–Aug Tue–Sat 9.30am–3.30pm; free), with its majestic 217ft (66m) steeple adapted from a Christopher Wren design. William Lloyd Garrison delivered his first anti-slavery speech here in 1829.

Next to the church on Tremont Street, pay your respects at the graves of Paul Revere, Samuel Adams, John Hancock,

King's Chapel Burying Ground

and other key revolutionary figures in the illustrious **Old Granary Burying Ground** ❻ (daily 9am–4pm, winter until 3pm), dating from 1660.

King's Chapel and Burying Ground
On the corner of School and Tremont streets is **King's Chapel** ❼ (tel: 617-523-1749; www.kings-chapel.org; Mon–Sat 10am–4pm, Sun 1.30–4pm; services Wed 6pm and Sun 11am; free). The present granite structure dates from 1754, but the chapel had its origins in the 1680s, when Britain's King James II made a colossal political blunder by sending to Boston a clergyman whose job was to install in the town the very thing the Puritans had hated and fled: a branch of the Church of England.

Next to the chapel, on Tremont Street, is Boston's first cemetery, **King's Chapel Burying Ground** (daily 9am–5pm, winter until 3pm), in use from 1630 to 1796. The Bay Colony's first governor, John Winthrop, was buried here in 1649.

Old City Hall
Farther along School Street is **Old City Hall** ❽ (tel: 617-523-8678; www.oldcityhall.com), built in 1865 in the French Second Empire style. When the city government decamped from here in 1969 for the new City Hall, this handsome edifice was preserved as a mixed-use complex of offices and a restaurant. In the forecourt are bronze statues of Benjamin Franklin and Josiah Quincy,

in his time a senator, Boston mayor and president of Harvard.

Old Corner Bookstore
At the intersection of School and Washington streets is the **Old Corner Bookstore** ❾, dating from 1712, and currently a Chipotle Mexican Grill restaurant. Over the years the building has served as an apothecary, a dry goods store, and a private residence, although it's fondly remembered in its 1828 incarnation as the home of the eminent Ticknor and Fields publishing firm and a bookstore. In the Golden Age of American literature, the store was a popular meeting place for John Greenleaf Whittier, Ralph Waldo Emerson, Harriet Beecher Stowe, Louisa May Alcott and other distinguished writers.

Old South Meeting House
Immediately to the right on Washington Street is the **Old South Meeting House** ❿ (tel: 617-482-6439; www.oldsouthmeetinghouse.org; Apr–Oct daily 9.30am–5pm, Nov–Mar daily 10am–4pm), built in 1727 and styled after the graceful London chapels of Sir Christopher Wren. It was at the Old South Meeting House that, on December 16, 1773, more than 5,000 Bostonians met to decide what to do with three tea-laden ships in the harbor. Disguised as Mohawk Indians, a gang of colonists, enraged at the British tax placed on tea and other imports, ran down Milk Street to Griffins Wharf. The crowd followed

Old City Hall

and, with cries of 'Boston harbor a tea-pot tonight!', 340 crates of tea were dumped overboard. The church was also the scene of the baptism on a chilly January 6, 1706, of Benjamin Franklin, born around the corner on Milk Street, where you will find the **Milk Street Café**, see ❶.

Old State House

From the Old South Meeting House continue north along Washington Street toward the junction with State Street. Immediately to the right, over-shadowed by modern skyscrapers, is the **Old State House** ⓫ (tel: 617-720-1713; www.bostonhistory.org; Sept–June daily 9am–5pm, July–Aug until 6pm), Boston's oldest public building, built in 1713 as the seat of the colonial government, and now a small museum displaying items relating to Boston's role in the Revolutionary War and other parts of the city's history.

Opposite the Old State House is the National Park Service Visitor Center (15 State Street; tel: 617-242-5642; www.nps.gov/bost; daily 9am–5pm), a valuable source of information and literature. Rangers lead free daily walking tours along part of the Freedom Trail from here.

Boston Massacre

It is easy to miss the circle of cobble-stones on a tiny traffic island at the junction of State and Congress streets. This marks the spot of the **Boston Massacre** ⓬, where on March 5, 1770, a handful of British soldiers fired into a jeering crowd that was pelting them with snowballs; five men were killed, including one former slave, Crispus Attucks, who is buried in the Old Granary Burying Ground.

Faneuil Hall and Quincy Market

Head north on Congress Street and turn right to reach **Faneuil Hall** ⓭ (tel: 617-242-5642; www.faneuilhall.com; daily 9.30am–4.30pm; free). A statue of Samuel Adams, one of the founding fathers of the United States, stands in front of the former public hall, which was named for benefactor Peter Faneuil. Designated by patriot orator James Otis as the 'Cradle of Liberty,' it was here that the Sons of Liberty called many meetings complaining about British taxation without representation. On the building's lower floors are many touristy shops, more of which you will find in the adjacent **Quincy Market** complex. The latter is named for Mayor Josiah Quincy, who came up with the idea for the 1826-vintage marketplace. Meat and produce were sold here for 150 years before the buildings were renovated to host the scores of souvenir stalls and boutiques found today.

Boston City Hall

On the west side of Congress Street climb the concrete steps leading up to **Boston City Hall** ⓮. Prior to the construction in 1969 of this charmless inverted ziggurat, the area was known

Celebrating a festa in the North End

as Scollay Square, a slightly disreputable entertainment area. In the 1960s the Boston Redevelopment Authority decided to raze Scollay Square and the nearby tenements of the West End. The area was renamed Government Center, its focus the vast, bleak City Hall Plaza.

New England Holocaust Memorial

Beautiful in a melancholy way are the six tall, slender glass-and-steel towers of the **New England Holocaust Memorial** ⑮ in Carmen Park, a strip of greenery opposite the City Hall between Union and Congress streets. Forming a mute tribute to those murdered by the Nazis in World War II, each glass column, wreathed in steam symbolizing the gas chambers, represents a different concentration camp and is inscribed with numbers – 6 million in total.

Weekend processions

If you are in Boston in summer, be sure to time your visit to the North End to catch one of the local Italian community's feasts or *festas*, celebrated in honor of saints' days. They are held almost every weekend in July and August, with Sunday being by far the more exciting day, and usually involve street fairs, brass bands, singers, raffles, food stalls selling sausage, peppers, and *zeppole* (fried dough), and processions in which saints' statues are carried, often festooned with contributions of paper money.

Blackstone Block

In stark contrast to the concrete wasteland of Government Center are the charming brick buildings and cobbled lanes, dating back to the 17th century, of **Blackstone Block** ⑯, named for Boston's first colonist, William Blackstone (who settled in the Boston Common area in 1625). The block is bounded by Union, Hanover, Blackstone, and North streets. At 41 Union Street is the historic **Union Oyster House**, see ②. Union Oyster House claims the title of Boston's oldest brick house. A rare example of Georgian architecture in the city, the restaurant dates to at least 1660, when it was owned by Boston's first town crier, William Courser. Mentioned in a city plan of 1708, the house was the office of the *Massachusetts* Spy newspaper from 1771 to 1775, while in 1776 the exiled Louis-Philippe, who later became king of France, taught French in the rooms above James Amblard's tailor shop.

A few yards down Marshall Street, opposite the 18th-century Ebenezer Hancock House at No. 10, look down to see the **Boston Stone**, a stone ball and trough built into the wall of a gift shop. Shipped from England in 1700 to serve as a paint mill, the stones were later used as the point from which all distances from Boston were measured. Their role as the hub of 'The Hub' was later taken over by the dome of the Massachusetts State House.

If it is a Friday or Saturday you may want to linger around here to enjoy the

North End rooves

New England Holocaust Memorial

fresh produce market that wraps its way around North and Blackstone streets. Otherwise, continue across the Rose Kennedy Greenway into the North End.

THE NORTH END

Until only a few years ago the raised expanse of the Fitzgerald Expressway (also known as the Central Artery) cut the North End off from the rest of the city. Now that the 'Big Dig' has buried the road underground, the cleared land forms a ribbon of parks through the city known collectively as the **Rose Kennedy Greenway** ⓱, named for the mother of President John F. Kennedy, who was born in the North End in 1890. Railings either side of Hanover Street, as it cuts through the park, are inscribed with historical dates and quotations about the area from past residents.

Paul Revere House

The North End is Boston's Little Italy, and the central artery Hanover Street is almost wall-to-wall cafés and restaurants. For an espresso to power your way, pause at **Caffé Paradiso**, see ❸, or **Caffé Vittoria**, see ❹.

Turn right on Richmond Street and then left to enter cobbled North Square. Here, at No. 19, you will find the **Paul Revere House** ⓲ (tel: 617-523-2338; www.paulreverehouse.org; mid-Apr–Oct daily 9.30am–5.15pm, Nov–mid-Apr daily 9.30am–4.15pm). Built in 1676, this two-story dwelling, with an overhanging second floor, is the oldest wooden house in downtown Boston. Revere, then a silversmith, took up residence in 1770, and it is furnished today much as it was when it was home to him and the first Mrs Revere, who bore him eight children, and then, when she died, to the second Mrs Revere, who produced a similar brood. It is from here that Revere started his historic horse ride that legendarily warned, 'the British are coming!'

Next door is the restored **Pierce-Hichborn House** (guided tours only once or twice daily; call Paul Revere House for details), which belonged to Nathaniel Hichborn, Revere's cousin. The asymmetrical, three-story brick building, built between 1711 and 1715 in the new English Renaissance style, was a radical departure from the Tudor-style wooden dwellings built in the previous century.

St Stephen's Church

Exit North Square via Prince Street following the red bricks of the Freedom Trail back to Hanover Street. Turn right and walk two blocks north to reach white-steepled **St Stephen's Church** ⓳. Built in 1804 as a Congregationalist Meeting House, this dignified structure is the only one of five Boston churches designed by noted Boston architect Charles Bulfinch that still stands.

Paul Revere Mall

Directly opposite St Stephen's Church is the **Paul Revere Mall** ⓴, known locally

St Stephen's Church

as the Prado. Built in 1933, this spacious brick courtyard is one of the liveliest public spaces in the North End – a sort of Americanized piazza where kids run around, old folks play cards, and footsore tourists take a breather from the Freedom Trail. In addition to a traditional Italian fountain, the Prado features a magnificent equestrian statue of Paul Revere, modeled in 1885 by Cyrus Dallin and cast in 1940. On the south (left) wall, bronze panels recall the history of Boston and its people.

Old North Church

At the far end of the Prado a small gate opens to the rear of Christ Church, more popularly known as **Old North Church** ㉑ (tel: 617-858-8231; www.oldnorth. com; June–Oct daily 9am–6pm, Nov–Dec and March–May daily 9am–5pm, Jan–Feb 10am–4pm; free). Built in 1723, this is Boston's oldest church. Its interior, painted white since 1912, sports high pew boxes, designed to keep in the warmth of braziers filled with hot coal or bricks, which were placed on the floor in winter. The clock at the rear and the four Baroque Belgian cherubs that surround it date back to the opening of the church. So does the organ case, although the actual instrument dates only from 1759. It is still played at the service every Sunday at 11am.

Copp's Hill Burying Ground

On exiting from the church, walk up Hull Street for about 150yds/m to **Copp's Hill Burying Ground** ㉒ (daily dawn–dusk), Boston's second-oldest cemetery (after King's Chapel), where the gravestones, some ornately carved, poke out of the grass like misshapen teeth. It is named for William Copp, who farmed on the hill's southeast slope in the mid-17th century. In the colonial period, the base of the hill, known pejoratively as New Guinea (after the African country of Guinea), was occupied by the city's first black community, and about 1,000 African-Americans are buried in the cemetery's northwest corner.

CHARLESTOWN

The Freedom Trail's red-brick route leads you down Hull Street to Commercial Street, where you turn left and then right to cross the Charles River on the **Charlestown Bridge** ㉓. Crossing the bridge (don't look down if you suffer from vertigo) provides an excellent view on the left-hand side of the **Charlestown Locks**, which control the water level between the river and the Inner Harbor, and, rising majestically in the background, the **Leonard P. Zakim Bunker Hill Bridge** (www.leonardpzakimbunker hillbridge.org), one of the most striking contemporary structures in the city.

Paul Revere Park

Below the bridge on the Charlestown side of the river is pretty little **Paul Revere Park** ㉔. Take the steps down to the park and follow the walkway

A gravestone in Copp's Hill Burying Ground

under the Charlestown Bridge and past the hotel on Tudor Wharf toward the Charlestown Navy Yard, before which you could take a breather at **Sorelle Bakery and Café**, see ⑤, facing onto **City Square** ㉕. In the square's center,

a small circle of greenery preserves the foundations of the Great House, a structure dating from 1629 and believed to have been John Winthrop's home and the colony's brief seat of government.

Charlestown Navy Yard
Back on Constitution Road, walk east toward the **Charlestown Navy Yard** ㉖, home to the USS *Constitution*. Just inside the entrance is the **Visitor Center** (tel: 617-242-5601; www.nps.gov/bost; daily Tue–Sun 9am–5pm), where you can find out about free tours of the ship and its neighbor, the restored naval destroyer USS *Cassin Young*.

The **USS *Constitution*** ㉗ (www.ussconstitutionmuseum.org; mid-Apr–mid-July Tue–Fri 2.30–6pm Sat–Sun 10am–6pm, Sept–early Nov Tue–Fri 2.30–5pm Sat–Sun 10am–5pm, mid-Nov–mid-Apr Thu–Fri 2.30–5pm Sat–Sun 10am–4pm; tours on the half-hour; donation welcome) is the world's oldest warship still in commission. It keeps this status thanks to an annual

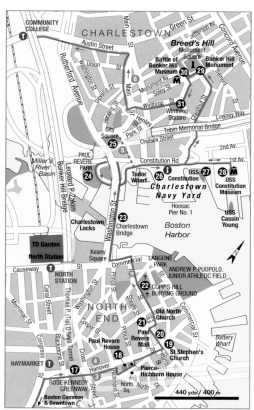

Clapboard houses in the Bunker Hill neighborhood

July 4 'turnaround,' when tugs pull 'Old Ironsides' out into the harbor.

Elsewhere in the Navy Yard is the **USS Constitution Museum** ㉘ (tel: 617-426-1812; www.ussconstitution museum.org; daily Apr–Oct 9am–6pm, Nov–Mar 10am–5pm; donation welcome), which simulates the experience of life below decks.

Bunker Hill Monument and Museum

Exit the Navy Yard back onto Constitution Road and turn right to reach Chelsea Street. Duck through the nearby underpass beneath the Tobin Bridge, emerging on Lowney Way. Turn left and then immediately right onto Chestnut Street. Continue along Chestnut Street

to the **Bunker Hill Monument** ㉙ (late Nov–late Apr daily 1–5pm, May–Oct daily 9am–5pm; free), a 220ft (67m) high granite obelisk crowning Breed's Hill. The battle was fought just north of the monument. Climb the 294 stairs to the top for rewarding views of the city.

On the corner of Monument Square and Monument Avenue is the small **Battle of Bunker Hill Museum** ㉚ (tel: 617-242-5641; www.nps.gov/bost; late Nov–late Apr daily 1pm–5pm, May–Oct 9am–5pm; free) where, on the second floor, hangs an excellent reproduction of the *Bunker Hill Cyclorama*, a circular painting that places the viewer at the heart of the battle's action.

Winthrop Square

From the southwest corner of Monument Square, head downhill along Winthrop Street into picturesque **Winthrop Square** ㉛. For a century this was a training field where Charlestown boys learned the art of war. At the northwest corner notice the gate flanked by bronze tablets commemorating those killed on June 17, 1775.

Return to Winthrop Street and keep going downhill, past the fire station and across Warren Street until you reach the junction with Main Street. Turn right here and continue to the corner of Pleasant Street, where the historic **Warren Tavern**, see ❻, dates from 1780. Both Paul Revere and George Washington once stayed here.

Charlestown history

Established in 1628, two years ahead of Boston, Charlestown lays claim to being the city's oldest neighbourhood. In 1630 it was the seat of the British government, and on Breed's Hill the bloody Battle of Bunker Hill was fought on June 17, 1775. Its prosperity used to be tied up with the Navy Yard founded in 1800. At times (usually wartimes) it was the busiest shipbuilding and repair yards in the US, but in 1974 demand had slowed to the point where the facility was forced to close – a third of it was taken over by the National Park Service.

All aboard the USS Constitution

From here, a short walk west along Austin Street and across busy Rutherford Avenue will bring you to Community College T Station, behind Bunker Hill Community College. Alternatively, amble back through Charlestown, admiring its many old homes, toward the North End, a pleasant place for an evening meal.

Food and drink

❶ MILK STREET CAFE

50 Milk Street; tel: 617-542-3663; www.milkstreetcafe.com; Mon–Fri 7am–3pm; $

Reasonable prices for generous portions is the deal at this kosher cafeteria with dairy and fish, but no meats. You can sample made-from-scratch dishes, such as roasted salmon salad and vegetable lasagne, and nutritious homemade soups.

❷ UNION OYSTER HOUSE

41 Union Street; tel: 617-227-2750; www.unionoysterhouse.com; daily 11am–9.30pm, Fri–Sat until 10pm; $$

A favorite haunt of President Kennedy, this touristy restaurant has a top-class raw bar, and serves both seafood and steaks in atmospheric rooms with creaky floors, low ceilings, and wooden booths.

❸ CAFFÉ PARADISO

255 Hanover Street, North End; tel: 617-742-1768; www.caffeparadisoboston.com; daily 7am–2am; $$

A popular local hangout, where the espressos, cannoli, panini, and calzones are all delicious. The television beams in soccer games from Italy via satellite.

❹ CAFFÉ VITTORIA

290–296 Hanover Street, North End; tel: 617-227-7606; www.caffevittoria.com; Sun–Thu 7am–midnight, Fri–Sat until 12.30am; $

This quintessential Italian café has quirky decor including almost a museum collection's worth of antique espresso machines. All kinds of beverages other than coffee are served along with traditional sweets.

❺ SORELLE BAKERY AND CAFÉ

100 City Square, Charlestown; tel: 617-242-5980; www.sorellecafe.com; Mon–Fri 7am–6pm, Sat–Sun 8am–6pm; $

This café serves incredible breads and pastries, fresh sandwiches and salads, and beverages.

❻ WARREN TAVERN

2 Pleasant Street, Charlestown; tel: 617-241-8142; www.warrentavern.com; Mon–Fri 11am–1am, Sat–Sun from 10am; $

Named for Revolutionary hero General Warren, this historic pub has low ceilings and beams that make it a convivial spot for lunch. Burgers and chunky sandwiches are the specialty. There is live music some evenings.

Widener Memorial Library

HARVARD

This walking tour takes you around the university's hallowed halls, into some of its excellent museums, ranging from visual arts to archaeology and natural history, and back across the river for fantastic views.

DISTANCE: 4 miles (6.5km)
TIME: A full day including museum visits
START/END: Harvard Square T Station
POINTS TO NOTE: It is difficult to do full justice to all of Harvard's museums in one day. Decide whether you would prefer a brief once-over of everything, or a concentrated session at, say, the natural history museums.

Many visitors associate Harvard with Boston, but the world-famous university is actually in the separate city of Cambridge, which lies on the north bank of the Charles River.

HARVARD YARD

Orientate yourself in **Harvard Square** ❶, which is actually an amorphous area rather than a four-sided square. To the west lies the Coop, or Harvard Cooperative Society (a bookstore and department store founded in 1882). To the east, **Harvard Yard** has the university's most historic buildings, bordered on the south and west by Massachusetts Avenue. The Yard is the geographic heart of America's oldest and most prestigious university, founded in 1636. Six of Harvard's graduates have become US president, and it has churned out dozens of Nobel and Pulitzer prize-winners.

'The Statue of Three Lies'

Enter Harvard Yard by the Johnston Gate, flanked on the right by **Massachusetts Hall** (1718) and on the left by **Harvard Hall**. Immediately ahead is **University Hall**, a white granite building designed by Charles Bulfinch in 1814. The bronze statue of John Harvard in front of University Hall is nicknamed 'The Statue of Three Lies,' because it is not of John Harvard, but of an 1884 undergraduate sculpted by Daniel French Chester; the inscription refers to John Harvard as founder of Harvard College, when he was in fact only the first major benefactor; and, contrary to the inscription, the college was not founded in 1638, the year of Harvard's bequest, but in 1636.

Students on the library steps

NEW YARD

Walk around University Hall into the Tercentenary Quadrangle, or **New Yard 2**, which, on the first Monday of each June, is the scene of Commencement, Harvard's major graduation ceremony.

New Yard is dominated on the south by the **Widener Memorial Library** (closed to general public), with its grand Corinthian colonnade atop a monumental flight of stairs. Inside lies the third-largest library in the country and part of the largest university library in the world – 13 million volumes including a Gutenberg Bible and a First Folio of Shakespeare.

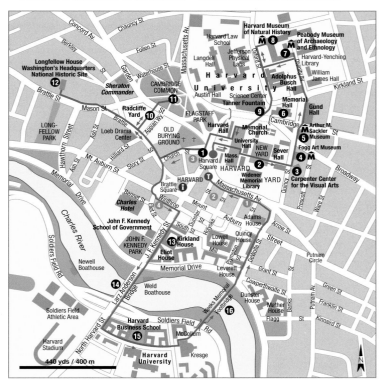

Butterflies in the Museum of Natural History

The north side of New Yard is punctuated by the soaring, delicate white spire of **Memorial Church**, which honors the Harvard dead in both world wars.

On the east side of the Yard is the Romanesque **Sever Hall**, considered one of architect H.H. Richardson's finest works. Its entrance is flanked by turreted towers, and the entire building is wonderfully rich in decorative brickwork.

ART MUSEUMS

Walk behind Sever Hall to emerge on Quincy Street, where you will find yourself facing the strikingly modern **Carpenter Center for the Visual Arts ❸** (tel: 617-496-5387; http://ccva.fas.harvard.edu; Thu–Sun 12–6pm; free), the only Le Corbusier building in North America. The ground-floor and third-floor galleries host exhibitions by international artists.

Next door at No. 32 are the **Fogg Art Museum** and **Busch-Reisinger Museum ❹**. The highlights of the Fogg include works by Ingres, and a fine collection of Pre-Raphaelite and French Impressionist works. In addition, there are dozens of Blake watercolors, and hundreds of Dürer and Rembrandt prints. The Busch-Reisinger collection, specializing in art from the German-speaking countries of central and northern Europe, includes 20th-century Expressionist canvases by Klee and Kandinsky, as well as the archives of architects Gropius and Feininger, forming the largest Bauhaus collection outside Germany.

Arthur M. Sackler Museum

The **Arthur M. Sackler Museum ❺** (485 Broadway; tel: 617-495-9400; www.harvardartmuseums.org; daily 10am–5pm) features an outstanding collection of Chinese jades. The Sackler's Ancient and Islamic collections are also noteworthy.

Either before or after visiting the Sackler, you can backtrack down Quincy Street to Massachusetts Avenue for lunch. Turn right to find **Mr Bartley's Burger Cottage**, see ❶, or walk further down the avenue, cross Harvard Square, and follow Brattle Street to Eliot Street to arrive at **b. good**, see ❷.

MEMORIAL HALL

Return to Quincy Street and follow it north across Cambridge Street. On the left is **Memorial Hall ❻**, a huge, redbrick Victorian Gothic pile with polychromatic roofs, dating from 1874, which contains the Sanders Theater, the university's largest auditorium. Its somewhat truncated appearance is the result of a fire that destroyed the tall pinnacled roof over the central tower. If the building is open, pop in to admire the stained-glass windows.

On the right of Memorial Hall is the contrasting slender-pillared **Gund Hall**, built in 1969, and home of the Graduate School of Design.

PEABODY MUSEUM

Cross Kirkland Street and enter Divinity Avenue. On the left side is the hand-

Memorial Hall   *The superb Peabody Museum*

some, medieval-style **Adolphus Busch Hall** (named for the beer baron). Toward the end of the avenue, on the left at No. 11, is the fascinating **Peabody Museum of Archaeology and Ethnology** ❼ (tel: 617-496-1027; www.peabody.harvard.edu; daily 9am–5pm). Among its superb collection of artifacts from around the globe are the only surviving Native American objects gathered by the explorers Meriwether Lewis and William Clark, who led the first American overland expedition to the Pacific coast (1804–6), as well as a huge photographic archive.

MUSEUM OF NATURAL HISTORY

Leaving the Peabody, turn right and right again to follow the footpath around the building to Oxford Street. Here, turn right once more to reach the entrance of the **Harvard Museum of Natural History** ❽ (tel: 617-495-3045; http://hmnh.harvard.edu; daily 9am–5pm). Its most famous exhibit is the collection of over 3,000 extraordinarily lifelike handmade glass flowers. Kids will also love its collection of dinosaur remains, including a 12ft (3.5m) tall Plateosaurus.

TANNER FOUNTAIN

Exit back onto Oxford Street, and, turning left, continue past the Science Center, the largest building on Harvard campus. In front of it, amid a patch of grass to the north of Harvard Yard, stands the unusual **Tanner Fountain** ❾, gurgling amid

a circular grouping of 159 boulders. Re-enter Harvard Yard and return to the Johnston Gate.

RADCLIFFE YARD

Cross Massachusetts Avenue and head west on Church Street. Turn right at the junction with Brattle Street. Continue walking until you pass Appian Way. Next on the right is **Radcliffe Yard** ❿, which is surrounded by a number of delightful late 19th- and early 20th-century buildings. This is where the renowned women's college of that name, now fully integrated with Harvard, began life in 1879.

Exit from the yard's far side onto Garden Street, which borders **Cambridge Common** ⓫. Surrounded by a semicircle of cannons, a bronze relief marks the spot

Harvard Tours

For the inside scoop on Harvard, take one of the student-led tours of the campus (see website for times; free), leaving from the Harvard University Information Center, Holyoke Center Arcade (1350 Massachusetts Avenue; tel: 617-495-1573; www.harvard.edu). A fun alternative is the 70-minute Hahvahd Tour by Trademark Tours (tel: 855-455-8747 ext 2; http://trademarktours.com; see website for times; donations welcome), which leaves from Harvard Square outside the Harvard Red Line Subway Station next to the Cambridge Information Kiosk.

On the banks of the Charles River

where, on July 4, 1775, George Washington assumed command of the Continental Army.

LONGFELLOW HOUSE

Return through Radcliffe Yard to Brattle Street. Leafy and tranquil compared to the hubbub of Harvard Square, this prestigious street is lined by splendid clapboard houses fronted by elegant porticoes, most from the 19th century, some from even earlier.

MIT

Harvard is not the only famous university in Cambridge. Hop on the T and emerge at Kendall/MIT station to explore the Massachusetts Institute of Technology (MIT). Founded in 1861, MIT's reputation for science research obscures the fact that there's a fair amount of support for the arts on campus too. The List Visual Arts Center (Wiesner Building, 20 Ames Street; tel: 617-253-4680; https://listart.mit.edu; Tue–Sun noon–6pm, Thu until 8pm; free) has temporary exhibits of outstanding contemporary art. In the west campus the Kresge Auditorium and the MIT Chapel are two outstanding buildings designed by a Finnish architect, Eero Saarinen, while in the east campus is the whimsical Frank Gehry-designed Ray and Maria Stata Center. Go inside to pick up a self-guided tour leaflet of the campus from the information desk.

The cream-colored clapboard building located at No. 105 is where Henry Wadsworth Longfellow (1807–82) composed many of his most famous works. It is now the **Longfellow House Washington's Headquarters National Historic Site** ⑫ (tel: 617-876-4491; www.nps.gov/long; late May–late Oct Wed–Sun noon–4.30pm). Even if the house is closed, its pleasant grounds are always open for inspection.

Stroll back along Brattle Street toward Harvard Square, pausing either at **L.A. Burdick Chocolate Shop and Café**, see ❸, or **The Red House**, see ❹, across Brattle Square on Winthrop Street.

TOWARD THE CHARLES RIVER

From Winthrop Street turn right onto John F. Kennedy Street, and walk south past, on the left, the neo-Georgian **Kirkland House** ⑬ and **Eliot House**. Each residential co-ed house is a small college with about 400 students and its own administration, library, dining hall, exclusive societies and clubs, and a veritable phalanx of tutors.

On the other side of John F. Kennedy Street is Harvard's **John F. Kennedy School of Government** (www.hks.harvard.edu), fronted by the riverside John F. Kennedy Park.

Across busy Memorial Drive the handsome **Larz Anderson Bridge** ⑭, named in memory of Nicholas Longworth Anderson, a distinguished colonel in the US Civil War, spans the Charles River. From

Longfellow House Washington's Headquarters National Historic Site

here, there are superb views of the college, and, in the foreground, the Weld Boathouse, home of Harvard's women's crew. The boathouse to the right is home to the men's crew.

HARVARD BUSINESS SCHOOL

Cross the river, and continue straight on what is now North Harvard Street for 100yds/m, passing on the right the Harvard playing fields and, on the left, the prestigious **Harvard Business School** ⓯. Turn left and stroll through the campus. Here the neo-Georgian buildings display a consistent rhythm of green doors, white window-frames, and red-brick walls.

Emerging on the school's east side, take the footbridge over busy Soldiers Field Road to the **Weeks Memorial Footbridge** ⓰, which again offers an excellent view of some of Harvard's residential buildings.

Cross Memorial Drive and head north along DeWolfe Street aiming for Massachusetts Avenue, where a left turn will bring you back to Harvard Square.

Food and drink

①　MR BARTLEY'S BURGER COTTAGE

1246 Massachusetts Avenue; tel: 617-354-6559; www.mrbartley.com; Tue–Sat 11am–9pm; $

A Harvard institution, this classic mom-and-pop burger joint offers a wide range of burgers named for celebrities like Beyoncé and Tom Brady

②　B. GOOD

1 Eliot Street; tel: 617-945-5485; www.bgood.com; Mon–Sat 11am–10pm, Sun 11am–9pm; $

Few restaurants can truly claim they serve healthy junk food, but B. Good actually does. Lean meats are hand-packed to create a variety of delicious burger combos, and there are hand-cut baked fries and excellent salads. Eat in or take out.

③　L.A. BURDICK CHOCOLATE SHOP AND CAFÉ

52 Brattle Street; tel: 617-491-4340; www.burdickchocolate.com; Sun–Thu 8am–9pm, Fri–Sat 8am–10pm; $

A quiet oasis removed from the bustle of Harvard Square. Indulge in an empty-calories meal of delectable handmade chocolates and pastries, accompanied by a great range of teas and coffees. Their hot chocolate is like a dessert in a cup.

④　THE RED HOUSE

98 Winthrop Street; tel: 617-576-0605; www.theredhouse.com; daily noon–11pm; $$

In a quaint, red-painted clapboard house, dating from 1802, this charming restaurant with a large outdoor deck serves most of its mains in half-portions – great if you're not so hungry or on a budget.

The clapboard Buckman Tavern

LEXINGTON AND CONCORD

Following the 'Battle Road' between Lexington and Concord,
west of Boston, will take you past key Revolutionary sites, as well
as the beautiful landscape that inspired American literary giants.

DISTANCE: 13 miles (20.5km) from Boston to Lexington; driving tour: 11 miles (18km)

TIME: A full day

START: National Heritage Museum, Lexington

END: Walden Pond, Concord

POINTS TO NOTE: By car you can visit all the sites in a day. Spend the night in Concord if you would like to linger at any of the museums or historic houses or hike the Battle Road Trail. Many places are closed Sunday morning and from November to March. If using public transportation, take bus 62 or 76 from Boston's Alewife T Station to Lexington center. From spring through fall, you can take the Liberty Ride tour between Lexington and Concord (see page 15). Otherwise, try Yellow Cab (tel: 781-862-4600). Commuter trains from Concord Depot take about 40 minutes to reach Boston's North Station. Salem (see page 50) is 23 miles (37km) east of Lexington.

LEXINGTON

To reach the start of this tour, drive out of Boston on Route 2. Turn right at exit 57 onto Route 4-225. As you approach the center of Lexington there are two sites of historical interest on the left.

Scottish Rite Masonic Museum & Library
Begin at the **Scottish Rite Masonic**

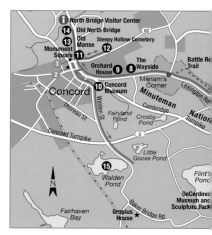

Detail of the Minuteman statue on Battle Green

Museum & Library ❶ (tel: 781-861-6559; www.srmml.org; Wed–Sat 10am–4pm; free), in a contemporary building entered on Marrett Road, which tells the story of freemasonry and fraternalism in American history.

Soon after is the 1635 **Munroe Tavern** ❷ (1332 Massachusetts Avenue; tel: 781-862-0295; www.lexingtonhistory. org; Apr–May Sat–Sun 10am–4pm, self- and guided tours), which served as headquarters for the Redcoats and as a hospital on their retreat from Concord.

Battle Green

Drive into the center and park. At one corner of the town common – a tiny triangular park known as **Battle Green** ❸ – stands the **Minuteman Statue**, honoring the 77 patriots who faced down the British here, igniting the American Revolution of 1775. They were called 'Minutemen' because they pledged to be ready to fight at a minute's notice.

Opposite on Bedford Street is **Buckman Tavern** ❹ (1 Bedford Street; tel: 781-862-5598; www.lexingtonhistory. org; Mar–Nov daily 9.30am–4pm, tours every half-hour), a clapboard building that has been restored to its original late 17th-century appearance. After the first battle of the Revolution, wounded Minutemen were brought here.

Hancock-Clarke House

A short walk northeast from Battle Green is **Hancock-Clarke House** ❺ (36 Hancock Street; tel: 781-861-0928; www. lexingtonhistory.org; Apr–May Sat–Sun 10am–4pm). Built in 1738, this house

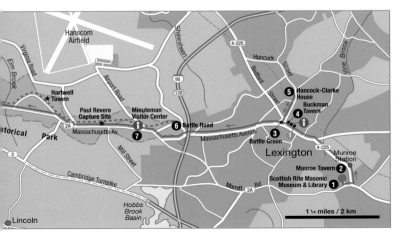

The Colonial Inn

is where, on the night of April 18, 1771, Paul Revere woke John Hancock and Samuel Adams with the warning that the British Army were coming.

Before leaving Lexington you could get some refreshments at **Via Lago**, see ❶.

BATTLE ROAD

From Battle Green, drive east on Massachusetts Avenue to join Route 2A which shadows **Battle Road** ❻, along which the British, harried by the Minutemen, marched towards Concord. This whole area is preserved in the Minuteman National Historical Park, through which runs an easy 5-mile (8km) **walking trail** (see dotted line on map). Stop off at the **Minuteman Visitor Center** ❼ (tel: 978-369-6993; www.nps.gov/mima; Apr–Oct daily 9am–5pm; free) to see an excellent multimedia presentation about the start of the Revolution.

CONCORD

The handsome small town of Concord is where the second engagement of the Revolution took place. During the first half of the 19th century a handful of renowned literati also lived here.

Literary homes

On the way into Concord is **The Wayside** ❽ (455 Lexington Road; tel: 978-318-7826; www.nps.gov/mima; guided tours mid-June–Oct Mon Thu–Sat 10am, 11am, 1pm, 2pm, 3pm, 4pm). Louisa

May Alcott and her family lived here, as did Nathaniel Hawthorne in later years. Most of the furnishings, though, date from the residence of Margaret Sidney, the author of the *Five Little Peppers*.

Down the road is delightful **Orchard House** ❾ (tel: 978-369-4118; www.louisamayalcott.org; Mon–Sat 10am–4.30pm [Nov–Mar Mon–Fri 11am–3pm], Sun 1–4.30pm), the Alcott family home from 1858 to 1877, where Louisa May wrote *Little Women* and her father, Bronson, founded his school.

Concord Museum to Sleepy Hollow

Where Lexington Road meets the Cambridge Turnpike (Route 2) is the splendid **Concord Museum** ❿ (tel: 978-369-9763; www.concordmuseum.org; Apr–Dec Mon–Sat 9am–5pm, Sun noon–5pm, June–Aug Sun 9am–5pm, Jan–Mar Mon–Sat 11am–4pm Sun 1–4pm). You can see Ralph Waldo Emerson's study, which was transferred from the Emerson House across the road. There are also artifacts associated with the author Henry Thoreau, including the writing desk from his Walden Pond abode.

Around 0.25 mile (400m) farther northwest is **Monument Square** ⓫, the heart of Concord. On the square's east side is **The Colonial Inn**, see ❷.

From the square, stroll east along Bedford Street to reach **Sleepy Hollow Cemetery** ⓬. In an idyllic setting in the northeast corner of the cemetery lies Authors' Ridge, the resting place of Hawthorne, the Alcotts, Emerson and Thoreau.

Firing a musket

Walden Pond

Old Manse

Return to Monument Square and drive north for about a mile (1.5km) on Monument Street to arrive at the **Old Manse** ⓭ (tel: 978-369-3909; www.thetrustees. org; mid-Mar–mid-May Sat–Sun noon–5pm, mid-May–Oct Tue–Sun noon–5pm, Nov–Dec Sat–Sun noon–5pm), set in immaculate grounds (free to visit). It was from this 1770 building that the Rev. William Emerson watched the battle in 1775 for the nearby Old North Bridge. It was later the residence of his grandson, Ralph Waldo Emerson, and then the Hawthornes.

Old North Bridge

From the Old Manse, walk to the replica **Old North Bridge** ⓮ across the Concord River. On the other side stands the **Minuteman statue**, rifle in one hand, ploughshare in the other. Emerson's immortal words 'The shot heard 'round the world' are inscribed on the plinth. On a hill overlooking the bridge is the **North Bridge Visitor Center** (tel: 978-369-6993; Apr–early Nov daily 9am–5pm).

Return to the center of Concord to find **Main Streets Market and Café**, see ❸. If driving, you could make a detour to **Walden Pond** ⓯. Drive south out of Concord along Walden Street, which crosses Route 2, for 1.5 miles (2.5km) to find Walden Pond (parking charge), which inspired Thoreau's memoir *Walden* (1854). It takes about an hour to circle the relatively small pond on foot. The best time to visit is in the fall. During summer the pond is a popular swimming spot. A cairn of stones stands alongside the site where the writer lived in a cabin between 1845 and 1847.

Food and drink

❶ VIA LAGO

1845 Massachusetts Avenue, Lexington; tel: 781-861-6174; www.vialagocatering.com; Mon–Wed 7am–9pm, Thu–Sat until 9.30pm; $
Freshly made sandwiches, light meals, and other snacks are available from this convivial café within sight of Battle Green.

❷ THE COLONIAL INN

48 Monument Square, Concord; tel: 978-369-9200; www.concordscolonialinn.com; daily 7am–9pm; $$

Dating back to 1716, this is as traditional as it gets in Concord. Meals are available all day, but book at least 48 hours in advance for their formal high tea, served Sat–Sun 3–4pm.

❸ MAIN STREETS MARKET AND CAFÉ

42 Main Street, Concord; tel: 978-369-9948; www.mainstreetsmarketandcafe.com; Mon–Thu 6.30am–10.30pm, Fri–Sat until 11.30pm, Sun until 9pm; $
A bustling self-serve hangout during the day, or grab a delicious cake and coffee to enjoy down at Walden Pond. There is live music here most evenings.

Replica of the Friendship at Derby Wharf

SALEM AND CAPE ANN

*Stroll around Salem, one of New England's most historic towns,
then use it as a base for exploring the rugged coves, fishing towns,
artists' colonies, and grand New England mansions of Cape Ann.*

DISTANCE: Salem to Rockport: 2.5
miles (38km); walking tour in Salem:
3.5 miles (5.5km)
TIME: Two days
START: Salem
END: Rockport
POINTS TO NOTE: Salem is 16 miles
(26km) north of Boston. Driving is the
best way of getting around Cape Ann;
the scenic coastal route follows MA
127 beyond Salem. However, Salem,
Gloucester, and Rockport can all be
reached by train from Boston's North
Station (see www.mbta.com). There's
also a ferry that connects Salem and
Boston from May to October (tel: 978-
741-0220; www.salemferry.com; one
way/round trip $25/45; 45 minutes),
and you can get around on Cape
Ann Transportation Authority buses
(www.canntran.com).

SALEM

Once one of the nation's great seaports,
Salem produced the country's first mil-

lionaires, and has the architectural and
cultural heritage to prove it in its McIntire
Historic District and the protected properties of the Peabody Essex Museum.
However, it does not take long to find
reminders of the activities most often
associated with the town – the trials and
executions of 'witches.'

The National Park Visitor Center (just
off Essex Mall on New Liberty Street; tel:
978-740-1650; www.nps.gov; May–Oct
daily 9am–5pm, Nov–Apr daily 10am–
5pm) is the place to pick up maps and
leaflets, consult the park rangers, and
watch an excellent 27-minute film about
the county's history. You can also find
useful information at www.salem.org.

Witch Dungeon Museum
Park your car near **Salem Station** and
walk down Washington Street, turning
right onto Lynde Street after two blocks. At
No. 16 is the **Witch Dungeon Museum ❶**
(tel: 978-741-3570; www.witchdungeon.
com; daily 10am–5pm; charge), where
you can watch a vividly staged reenact-
ment of a trial, adapted from a 1692 man-
uscript, before being guided through the

House of the Seven Gables

tiny dank dungeons in which the accused were held.

Witch House

The spooky wooden house on the corner of Essex and North streets is the **Witch House ❷** (tel: 978-744-8815; mid-May–Nov daily 10am–5pm; charge), where trial magistrate Jonathan Corwin cross-examined more than 200 suspected witches; the decor is authentic to the period.

McIntire Historic District

Named for Samuel McIntire (1757–1811), one of the foremost American architects of his day, this historic area of Salem, roughly bounded by Federal, Flint, Broad, and Summer/North Streets, showcases four centuries of architectural styles.

Backtrack from the Witch House to Federal Street, where at No. 80 stands the McIntire-designed **Peirce-Nichols House ❸** (c.1782); its east parlor has

been restored and is open for tours by arrangement with the Peabody Essex Museum (see page 52).

Return to Essex Street and proceed to No. 318, the Georgian-period **Ropes Mansion ❹**, which stands in a beautiful garden and features a rare collection of Nanking porcelain and Irish glass.

Turn into quaint Botts Court and walk to Chestnut Street, one of Salem's finest thoroughfares. At no. 34 is the fine **Phillips House ❺** (tel: 978-744-0440; www.historicnewengland.org; June–Oct Tue–Sun 11am–4pm, Nov–May Sat–Sun 11am–4pm, tours every half-hour), where the carriage house contains several antique cars. Retrace your steps back along Chestnut Street, and continue to No. 9, the red-brick Federalist gem **Hamilton Hall ❻** (tel: 978-744-0805; www.hamiltonhall.org; Mon–Fri 9am–noon; free).

From the corner of Chestnut Street, turn left onto Summer Street and then

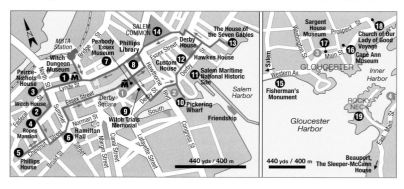

The Custom House

right at Essex Street to reach the pedestrian Essex Mall, recognizable by the red paving that matches the red bricks of the buildings. Turn right onto Central Street to find **Red's Sandwich Shop**, see ❶.

Peabody Essex Museum

Back on the mall, reserve a decent block of time to visit the outstanding **Peabody Essex Museum** ❼ (tel: 978-745-9500; http://pem.org; Tue–Sun 10am–5pm), where an impressive contemporary building by Moshe Safdie displays a fraction of the collection of nearly a million objects.

The museum's origins date back to 1799 and to the art and antiques amassed by Salem's seafaring merchants on their global travels. Ships'

models, figureheads, nautical instruments, charts and maps abound, but the museum also has fine antiques from China, Japan and India, as well as plenty of artifacts from the South Pacific (especially the Solomon Islands) and further afield. There's also a 200-year-old Chinese merchant's home, transported from China and rebuilt as part of the museum; entry to this is by timed ticket and advance reservations are advised.

Diagonally opposite the Peabody Essex Museum, a mini architectural park surrounds the red-brick **Phillips Library** ❽ (tel: 978-745-9500; http://pem.org; Wed–Thu 10am–4.30pm; free), which has a lovely reading room. Notice the stark contrast between the massive columns of the **Andrew-Safford House** (1819; 13 Washington Square) and, behind it, the tiny features of the **Derby-Beebe Summerhouse** (1799). Also here are the **Gardner-Pingree House** (1804; 128 Essex Street) and, from 1727, the neighboring **Crowninshield-Bentley House**.

On leaving the Peabody, follow the short footpath around its side until you reach Charter Street. Here, next to the Burying Point Cemetery – resting place of witch judge John Hathorne – is the most poignant of all Salem's witch-connected sites. The **Witch Trials Memorial** ❾, dedicated by Holocaust survivor and renowned writer Elie Wiesel in 1992, is a contemplative space surrounded by 20 stone benches etched with the trial victims' names, and shaded by a clump of

The Peabody Essex Museum displays all kinds of maritime artifacts

black locust trees – reputedly the kind from which the convicted were hanged.

Salem Maritime National Historic Site

From the cemetery, cross Derby Street and walk along its south side toward **Pickering Wharf** ⑩, a touristy collection of stores, restaurants, and antiques shops. The best place to eat around here is **Finz**, see ②.

Next to the wharf, the **Salem Maritime National Historic Site** ⑪ focuses on Salem's port. Stop by the **Orientation Center** (tel: 978-740-1650; www. nps.gov; daily 9am–5pm) to find out about ranger-guided tours (charge) and the nearby Custom House, Derby House, and Narbonne House, as well as the *Friendship of Salem*, a full-scale replica of a 1797 three-masted East India merchant ship. It is docked at Derby Wharf, which is one of the few wharves that remain from the 40 of Salem's heyday.

Custom House

Facing the wharf is the **Custom House** ⑫ (1819), surmounted by a gilded eagle clutching arrows and a shield in its claws, which was made famous by Nathaniel Hawthorne. Salem's most famous son worked here for three years of 'slavery,' on which he based the introduction of *The Scarlet Letter* (1850).

Adjacent to the Custom House is the **Hawkes House** (1780; not open to the public) and, beyond that, the ochre-brick **Derby House** (1761). The former was built by shipowner Elias Hasket Derby (probably America's first millionaire) to replace the latter, but it was used as a storehouse for booty taken by his Revolutionary privateers.

The House of the Seven Gables

Continue down Derby Street from the Custom House to reach, at No. 115, **The House of the Seven Gables** ⑬ (tel: 978-744-0991; www.7gables.org; June Sun–Thu 10am–5pm Fri–Sat until 7pm, July–Oct daily 10am–7pm, Nov–Dec daily 10am–5pm, mid-Jan–mid-Feb Fri–Tue 10am–5pm, mid-Feb–May daily 10am–5pm), which inspired Hawthorne to write the 1851 novel of the same name. The small house in which he was born in 1806 has been moved into the grounds. Guides will lead you through rooms stuffed with period furniture. Take a breather in the lovely garden afterwards.

Return to the town center by walking via **Salem Common** ⑭, where you will find the historic **Hawthorne Hotel** (see page 100), an ideal base for the night.

GLOUCESTER

Take the coastal route MA 127 northeast out of Salem and continue on for 16 miles (26km) to **Gloucester**. Founded in 1623, it is the nation's oldest seaport. Unlike Salem, its harbor is still fairly active (although not as busy as it used to be), with many fishermen now of Portuguese or Italian descent.

On the way into town, just over the drawbridge spanning the Annisquam

Gloucester harbor at dusk

Canal stands the **Fisherman's Monument** ⑮, depicting a helmsman gripping a wheel as he scans the horizon. Those familiar with the book and film *The Perfect Storm*, about an ill-fated Gloucester crew, will know that the poignancy of this memorial to those who have perished at sea is not merely a matter of ancient history.

Town Walk

Begin an exploration of the town at the **Cape Ann Museum** ⑯ (27 Pleasant Street; tel: 978-283-0455; www.cape annmuseum.org; Tue–Sat 10am–5pm, Sun 1–4pm), displaying seascapes by the renowned American maritime painter Fitz Hugh Lane, and an interesting collection of furniture, silver, and porcelain, in the handsome home of Captain Elias Davis (1804) and the adjoining White-Ellery House (c.1709).

The **Sargent House Museum** ⑰ (tel: 978-281-2432; http://sargenthouse. org; June–Aug Fri–Sun noon–last tour at 3pm) is a short walk west along Middle Street at No. 49. The home of Judith Sargent Murray, an early advocate of women's rights, recreates the decor of 1782 when the house was built. A block south, toward the harbor, you will find several lunch options on Main Street, including **Passports**, see ③.

Walk east on Main Street for 500m/ yds and turn left on Prospect Street for the attractive Portuguese **Church of Our Lady of Good Voyage** ⑱, recognizable by its two blue cupolas.

Rocky Neck and Eastern Point

Now drive around the harbor to East Main Street, passing **Duckworth's Bistrot**, see ④, and heading on to **Rocky Neck** ⑲ (www.rockyneckartcolony.org), the oldest artists' colony in the US, in a wonderful coastal setting. Rudyard Kipling worked on *Captains Courageous* (1897), about Gloucester fishermen, while staying here.

On leaving Rocky Neck, turn right onto Eastern Point Road. After about 1 mile (1.5km), take the right fork, even though it's marked 'private.' This is the exclusive enclave of Eastern Point, which has a score of magnificent homes. Open to the public is **Beauport, the Sleeper-McCann House** ⑳ (tel: 978-283-0800; www.historicnewengland.org; June–mid-Oct Tue–Sat 10am–last tour at 4pm), which as built and furnished between

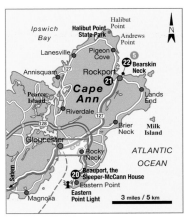

Colourful fishing floats

1907 and 1934 by Henry Davis Sleeper, a collector of American art and antiquities.

ROCKPORT

About 7 miles (11km) northeast of Gloucester is picturesque **Rockport** ㉑, once a shipping center for locally cut granite. In the 1920s Rockport was discovered by artists and remains an art colony today. A dozen or so galleries display works of both local and international artists on Main Street, but what attracts most tourists is **Bearskin Neck** ㉒. This narrow peninsula, jutting out beyond the harbor, is densely packed with tiny dwellings and old fishing sheds, now converted into galleries, antiques stores, and restaurants. Enjoy magnificent views of the Atlantic from the breakwater, just before which you will pass **My Place by the Sea**, see ❺.

Food and drink

❶ RED'S SANDWICH SHOP
15 Central Street; tel: 978-745-3527; www.redssandwichshop.com; Mon–Sat 5am–3pm, Sun 6am–1pm; $
A Salem breakfast institution housed in the old London Coffee House, dating from 1698. Arrive early if you don't want to stand in line.

❷ FINZ
76 Wharf Street; tel: 978-744-8485; ww.hipfinz.com; daily 11.30am–10pm Fri–Sat until 11pm; $–$$
The best place to enjoy seafood overlooking Salem Harbor. Bypass the lobster roll in favor of the excellent salmon wrap or great-value haddock sandwich.

❸ PASSPORTS
110 Main Street, Gloucester; tel: 978-281-3680; http://passportsgloucester.com; Mon–Fri 11.30am–9pm, Sat–Sun 10am–9pm; $

Ideal for lunch or a quick snack, this romantically themed café has local artwork covering the walls and does great salads, soups, and seafood.

❹ DUCKWORTH'S BISTROT
197 East Main Street, Gloucester; tel: 978-282-4426; www.duckworthsbistrot.com; Tue–Thu 5–9.30pm, Fri–Sat 4–9.30pm; $$
A great place to return for dinner after a day's outing around Cape Ann. Chef Ken Duckworth's modern American cuisine uses the best of local produce. Many dishes, such as grilled organic chicken and sautéed veal cutlets, also come in half-portions.

❺ MY PLACE BY THE SEA
68 Bearskin Neck, Rockport; tel: 978-546-9667; www.myplacebythesea.com; daily 11.30am–9pm; $$
Fantastic views are guaranteed at this friendly place that serves imaginative modern American cuisine. It is good value for lunch, but pricier for dinner, when reservations are advised.

A quiet Cape Cod village

SOUTH SHORE AND CAPE COD

This road trip down the shoreline along which New England was founded links historic Plymouth with laid-back Provincetown at the tip of Cape Cod, via pretty coastal villages and national park-protected dunes and beaches.

DISTANCE: 78 miles (125km)
TIME: Two to three days
START: Plymouth
END: Provincetown
POINTS TO NOTE: Plymouth is a 40-mile (64km) drive south of Boston along I-93, then Route 3. There are direct MBTA trains to Plymouth, but the service is limited; instead, take one of the more frequent trains to Kingston, from where Gatra buses (tel: 1-800-483-2500; www.gatra.org) run to Plymouth's center. Plymouth and Brockton buses (tel: 508-746-0378; www.p-b.com) run from Boston to Plymouth's bus depot, just off Route 3, around 2 miles (3km) southwest of Plymouth Rock; they also offer services to Provincetown via Hyannis. From May–Oct several daily ferries run between Boston and Provincetown, taking 1.5 hours one-way; see www.boston harborcruises.com and www.baystate cruisecompany.com for details. Many places in Provincetown are closed mid-Dec–mid-Mar. Providence is 42.5 miles (68km) west of Plymouth on Route 44.

Despite all the fuss made over Plymouth Rock, history relates that Plymouth was not the Pilgrim Fathers' first landfall in the New World. That honor belongs to Provincetown at the tip of Cape Cod, where a small party landed on November 21, 1620. Walking tours around these two historic towns bookend a road trip that passes through other attractive pit stops along the cape.

PLYMOUTH

Park near the **Waterfront Tourist Information Center** Center (130 Water Street; tel: 800-872-1620; www.seeply mouth.com; Apr–May and Sept–Oct 9am–5pm, June–Aug 8am–8pm), and walk south along Water Street towards **Pilgrim Memorial State Park**. Its focus is **Plymouth Rock ❶**, identified in 1741 by a third-generation elder of the Plymouth Church as the rock on which the Pilgrim Fathers first stepped, in December 1620, on reaching America.

Nearby is the ***Mayflower II* ❷** (tel: 508-746-1622; www.plimoth.org; Apr–Nov daily 9am–5pm), a replica of the origi-

The Mayflower II   *Empty dunes on the cape's seashore*

nal *Mayflower*, built in England and sailed to Plymouth in 1957. The vessel vividly conveys the hardships that the 102 members of the crew suffered during the original 55-day voyage. The ship is away at Mystic Seaport receiving a full restoration until 2019.

Beside the Town Brook

Follow Water Street south to **Brewster Gardens ❸**, which hugs both sides of the **Town Brook** from which the first Native Americans and, later, the British settlers got their fresh water and herring.

Cross the wooden bridge and follow the brook under two road bridges to arrive at **Plimoth Grist Mill ❹** (6 Spring Lane; tel: 508-746-1622; www.plimoth. org; Apr–Nov daily 9am–5pm), located on the site of the mill established in 1636 by John Jenney. Corn is still ground here as it was in the Pilgrims' time.

Turn right off Spring Lane onto Summer Street to find, at No. 42, the oldest home in Plymouth. The **Richard Sparrow House ❺** (tel: 508-747-1240; www. sparrowhouse.com; daily 10am–5pm) dates from 1640 and is set up so you can see how the early settlers lived.

Mayflower Society House

Follow Summer Street, turn left on Market Street and walk through the Town Square to Main Street, Plymouth's central shopping street, where you will find **Kiskadee Coffee Company**, see ❶. Take the second right onto North Street, along which is the whitewashed 1754 **Mayflower Society House ❻** (tel: 508-746-3188; www. themayflowersociety.com; mid-May–October daily 11am–4pm). Tours of the interior reflect the occupants down the centuries,

[MAP]

Town Wharf

Waterfront Visitor Information Center ❶

Plymouth Harbor

220 yds / 200 m

N

Memorial Dr.
Water Street
Chilton St.
M Pilgrim Hall Museum ❼
Court Street
Howland St.
Brewster St.
Winslow St.
Water St.

Mayflower II (Gone-until 2019) ❷

State Pier ❷
PILGRIM MEMORIAL STATE PARK

Plymouth Rock ❶

Mayflower Society House ❻

Main Street
North Street
Spooner House
Middle St.
Massasoit
Cole's Hill

Sever St.
Allerton St.
North Russell St.
South Russell St.
School St.

BURIAL HILL †
First Church of Plymouth †
Church of the Pilgrimage ❸
Town Square
Church St.
Court House
Leyden St.
BREWSTER GARDENS ❸
Union St.
Water St.
Brook
Bradford St.

Richard Sparrow House ❺

Market St.
Town Brook
Spring La.
Jabez Howland House

Summer St.
Robinson St.
Sagamore St.
Pleasant St.
VILLAGE GREEN
Sandwich St.

Willard Place

Plimoth Grist Mill ❹

Plimoth Plantation ❽

Native American dress at the Wampanoag Homesite

while behind the house is a library for genealogical research.

Return to Main Street and continue north along Court Street to the 1824 **Pilgrim Hall Museum** ❼ (tel: 508-746-1620; www.pilgrimhall.org; mid-Feb–Dec daily 9am–4.30pm), which features an extensive collection of memorabilia from the first Pilgrim families, a range of Native American artifacts and the remains of *Sparrow Hawk*, a sailing ship that was wrecked in 1626.

Turn right down Memorial Drive to arrive back at the Tourist Information Center. Across the road is the Town Wharf and **Lobster Hut**, see ❷.

PLIMOTH PLANTATION

It is 2.5 miles (4km) southeast from the center of Plymouth to the **Plimoth Plantation** ❽ (137 Warren Avenue; tel: 508-746-1622; www.plimoth.org; mid-Mar–Nov daily 9am–5pm), where the year is always 1627; they use the 17th-century phonetic spelling for Plymouth, as Governor William Bradford did in his diary. In the plantation's English Village actor-guides dressed in authentic 17th-century costumes and speaking in old English dialects portray historical residents of the colony, salting fish, shearing sheep, and baking bread in clay ovens. The **Wampanoag Homesite** shows how Native Americans lived in Massachusetts in the 1620s, and is a rare chance to meet native people in traditional dress and find out about their ancient culture and skills.

UPPER CAPE

Around 15 miles (24km) south of Plymouth, Route 3 crosses the Cape Cod Canal via the Sagamore Bridge. From here, follow the old King's Highway (Route 6A) which hugs the western coastline of the Upper Cape as it winds its way through a series of pretty villages.

Sandwich

The first major one you will come to is **Sandwich** ❾. The **Sandwich Glass Museum** (129 Main Street; tel: 508-888-0251; www.sandwichglassmuseum.org; Apr–Dec 9.30am–5pm, Feb–Mar Wed–Sun 9.30am–4pm) celebrates the town's 19th-century glassmaking history with rooms of colored glassware as well as glassblowing demonstrations.

Head south on Grove Street to find the **Heritage Museums and Gardens** (tel: 508-888-3300; www.heritagemuseums andgardens.org; mid-Apr–mid-Oct daily 10am–5pm). There is something for everyone in its beautifully landscaped 100-acre (40ha) grounds, with galleries showing folk art, militaria, and old automobiles, plus a working carousel from 1912 that kids will adore.

Yarmouth and Brewster

The flavor of this unspoiled corner of the cape is typified in **Yarmouth Port** ❿, 15 miles (24km) east of Sandwich, where the handsome 1840 Greek Revival **Captain Bangs Hallet House** (11 Strawberry Lane; tel: 508-362-3021; http://

Glassblowing at Sandwich   *1627 English Village at Plimoth Plantation*

capecodmuseumtrail.com; June–mid-Oct Thu–Sun tours at 1, 2 and 3pm) has its parlours arranged as if the captain was just back from a voyage to China; out back, nature trails crisscross 50 acres (20ha) of meadow and woods.

At **Brewster ⑪**, 12 miles (19km) farther east, there are more trails to explore at the **Cape Cod Museum of Natural History** (869 Main Street; tel: 508-896-3867; www.ccmnh.org; June–Aug daily 9.30am–4pm, Sept 11am–3pm, Oct–mid-Dec Apr–May Wed–Sun 11am–3pm), as well as exhibits about the cape's flora and fauna.

LOWER CAPE

The confusingly named 'Lower Cape,' the outer part, begins at **Orleans**, 5

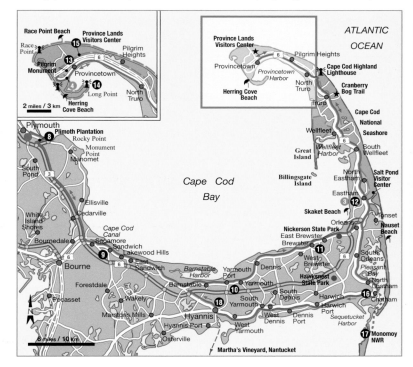

Provincetown Art Association & Museum

miles (8km) past Brewster. Not far from the town's busy traffic circle are two fine beaches – **Nauset** (Beach Road) on the colder, rougher Atlantic ocean side, and **Skaket** (Skaket Beach Road), which has calm bay frontage.

Follow Route 6 for 3 miles (5km) north to **Eastham** ⓲, home to the lobster shack **Arnold's**, see ❸, and the **Cape Cod National Seashore's Salt Pond Visitor Center** (Nauset Road; tel: 508-255-3421; daily 9am–4.30pm), with exhibits about the dune lands that stretch north for 30 miles (48km) along the Great Beach to Provincetown, 19 miles (31km) farther along Route 6.

PROVINCETOWN

Thick with antiques, crafts and souvenir shops, art galleries, cafés, restaurants, and bars, **Provincetown** ⓳, or 'P-town,' is an unashamed tourist destination, but also, thanks to strict town ordinances, a beautiful-looking one. It's no surprise that generations of artists have been drawn to P-town and continue to practice here. There is also a lively gay scene.

Entering P-town along the one-way Commercial Street from the south, you will first hit the **East End**, packed with galleries as well as, at No. 460, the **Provincetown Art Association & Museum** (PAAM; tel: 508-487-1750; www.paam.org; June 11am–5pm, July–Aug Mon–Thu 11am–8pm Fri 11am–10pm Sat 11am–6pm Sun 11am–5pm, Sept Mon–Thu and Sat 11am–6pm Fri until 10pm

Sun until 5pm, Oct–May Thu–Sun noon–5pm). Top-class exhibitions are staged here, maintaining a tradition that started in 1899 with the founding of the Cape Cod School of Art by Charles Hawthorne.

Pilgrim Monument
The Pilgrim Fathers anchored in Provincetown before heading off to Plymouth, an event commemorated by the 252ft (77m) **Pilgrim Monument and Provincetown Museum** (High Pole Hill Road; tel: 508-487-1310; www.pilgrim-monument.org; Apr–May and mid-Sept–Nov daily 9am–5pm, June–mid-Sept daily 9am–7pm). To get your bearings of P-town's confusing geography, and for a grand 360-degree view of the Lower Cape, it is worth slogging up the tower's 116 steps and 60 ramps.

Farther down Commercial Street past a smattering of antiques shops, follow the road left around the Coast Guard Station to the **West End** of town, where weatherboard buildings are surrounded by lovely flower gardens. Particularly picturesque is the **Red Inn**, see ❹.

Cape Cod National Seashore
Provincetown's best beaches are part of the **Cape Cod National Seashore** (CCNS), which includes **Long Point** ⓴, the slender sandbar that hooks back into Cape Cod Bay. You can reach here by walking across the breakwater at the far west end of Commercial Street; the uneven stones can make the crossing a challenge. Once on Long Point you can aim either right to the lighthouse at Wood End

Chatham windmill

Race Point Beach

or left to the lighthouse on the tip of the sandbar – going in this direction you will pass the P-town nudist beach.

A fine view of the area can be had from the observation deck above the **Province Lands Visitors Center** ⑮ (tel: 508-487-1256; www.nps.gov/caco; mid-Apr–mid-Oct daily 9am–5pm; free), where you can find out about ranger-led walks around the national park. Note if you bring your car or bike into the national park area, there is a small charge.

RETURN TO UPPER CAPE

As you journey towards Boston or head on to Providence (see page 66), check out the Atlantic Coast side of the cape. From Orleans, continue south for 7 miles (11km) on Route 28 to upscale **Chatham** ⑯, where you watch the fishing fleet return to the Fish Pier in the late afternoon, or take a boat ride to the 2,700-acre (6,670ha) **Monomoy National Wildlife Refuge** ⑰ (tel: 508-945-0594; www.fws.gov/refuge/monomoy), a haven for birds and seals.

Hyannis
Route 28 back to the mainland passes through the busiest and most developed part of the cape. The main stop along this stretch is **Hyannis** ⑱ (19 miles/31km west of Chatham), which is famous as the summer residence of the Kennedy family. Here you can catch a ferry to **Martha's Vineyard** or **Nantucket** (tel: 800-492-8082; https://hylinecruises.com).

Food and drink

❶ KISKADEE COFFEE COMPANY
18 Main Street; tel: 508-830-1410; daily 7.30am–6pm; $
They do coffee, of course, but also a big range of bagel and panini sandwiches.

❷ LOBSTER HUT
25 Town Wharf; tel: 508-746-2270; www.lobsterhutplymouth.com; Sun–Thu 11am–7pm, Fri–Sat until 8pm; $
Nothing fancy, but when it comes to enjoying seafood within toe-dipping distance of the water then this institution is the place to be.

❸ ARNOLD'S
3580 State Highway/Route 6, Eastham; tel: 508-255-2575; www.arnoldsrestaurant.com; mid-May–mid-June Fri–Sun 11.30am–8pm, mid-June–early Oct daily until 9pm; $–$$
A long-running lobster and clam bar that also serves award-winning ice cream and has a fun mini-golf course to entertain the kids.

❹ RED INN
15 Commercial Street, Provincetown; tel: 508-487-7334; http://theredinn.com; May–Oct daily 5.30pm–late, Fri–Sun 11.30am–3pm, Nov–early Dec Sat–Sun 5.30pm–late; $$$
One of the most pleasant places to dine in P-town, this elegant West End inn has beautiful gardens and a prime beachside position. The cuisine is modern American and the portions are generous.

Ashley House in Historic Deerfield

THE BERKSHIRES AND PIONEER VALLEY

Towns such as Stockbridge, Lenox, and North Adams in the gently rolling hills of west Massachusetts are among the venues for art galleries, renowned summer music festivals, and the splendor of fall foliage.

DISTANCE: 184 miles (296km)
TIME: Two to three days
START/END: Springfield
POINTS TO NOTE: Springfield is 90 miles (145km) west of Boston and connected to it by Amtrak trains. It is 65 miles (105km) south to New Haven and 60 miles (97km) north to Brattleboro. See www.berkshires.org and www.valleyvisitor.com.

While Massachusetts's Berkshire Hills are far less rugged than the mountains of Vermont and New Hampshire, they do incorporate a variety of scenery. Benefiting from their proximity to Boston and New York, they have long been a favorite countryside escape for urbanites and artists, such as Norman Rockwell, who made Stockbridge his home. The area has also become famous for its summer roster of high-profile arts festivals.

SPRINGFIELD

The **Pioneer Valley**, named for the 17th-century settlers of the area, forms the eastern gateway to the region, where the largest city is **Springfield ❶**.

Begin in the reasonably handsome and busy downtown area by exploring the five institutions that make up **Springfield Museums** (21 Edwards Street; tel: 413-263-6800; www.springfieldmuseums.org; Tue–Sat 10am–5pm Sun 11am–5pm). The **Connecticut Valley Historical Museum** focuses on local history; the **George Walter Vincent Smith Art Museum** is strong in Japanese art, armor, and decorative items; the **Michele and Donald D'Amour Museum of Fine Arts** exhibits American and French Impressionist works; the **Springfield Science Museum** (Tue–Sat 10am–5pm, Sun 11am–5pm) has interactive displays; and the new **Museum of Springfield History** looks at the city's development as a manufacturing center. In the Quadrangle, bronze sculptures of beloved characters make up the delightful **Dr Seuss Sculpture Garden** (www.catinthehat.org; free), honoring the city's famous children's book writer. A short walk south of the museums is **Nadim's Downtown Mediterranean Restaurant**, see ❶.

Walking in the Berkshires

Springfield Armory National Historic Site

Armory and Basketball Museums

Due to its location on the conveniently navigable Connecticut River, Springfield was selected as the site of the first US arsenal. Ten minutes' walk north of the Springfield Museums is the **Springfield Armory National Historic Site** (1 Armory Square; tel: 413-734-8551; www.nps.gov/spar; June–Oct daily 9am–5pm, Nov–May Wed–Sun daily 9am–5pm; free), which tells the story of nearly 200 years of armament manufacturing.

Beside the Riverfront Park is the state-of-the-art **Naismith Memorial Basketball Hall of Fame** (1000 West Columbus Avenue; tel: 877-446-6752; www.hoophall.com; daily 10am–4pm), named for Dr James Naismith, who invented the sport in 1891 in Springfield.

THE BERKSHIRES

Stockbridge

Follow I-90 west from Springfield for 48 miles (77km) to **Stockbridge ②**, where the artist Norman Rockwell (1894–1978), chronicler of American life, lived for 25 years. Main Street looks much as it did when Rockwell painted it back in the 1960s, save for the weird and wonderful

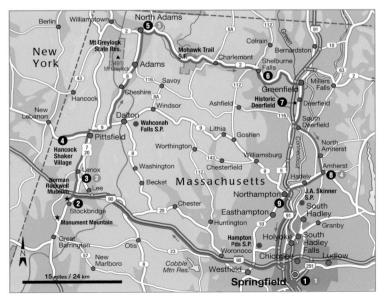

Norman Rockwell's studio

sculptures that dot the town in a festival held each year from June–October.

To see original paintings by Rockwell – more vivid than the magazine covers they became – and his charming studio, drive 2 miles (3km) to the **Norman Rockwell Museum** (9 Glendale Road, Route 183; tel: 413-298-4100; www.nrm.org; May–Oct daily 10am–5pm, Nov–Apr Mon–Fri 10am–4pm, Sat–Sun 10am–5pm).

The other estate worth seeing in the area is that of the sculptor Daniel Chester French, who created the Lincoln Memorial in Washington DC and the Minuteman statue in Concord. At **Chesterwood** (4 Williamsville Road; tel: 413-298-3579; www.chesterwood.org; June–mid-Oct daily 10am–5pm), a mile (1.5km) to the west, you can see his plaster casts and models in the Barn Gallery, as well as explore the formal gardens and woodland paths designed by French himself.

Lenox

Eight miles (13km) north of Stockbridge on Route 7A is the quintessential Berkshires village of **Lenox ❸**, home to the summer **Tanglewood Music Festival** (see page 25) and the **Haven Café and Bakery**, see ❷. Celebrated author Edith Wharton (1862–1937) built her Georgian Revival summer residence **The Mount** (2 Plunkett Street; tel: 413-551-5111; www.edithwharton.org; mid-May–Oct daily 10am–5pm) in Lenox in 1902. Three acres (1.2ha) of lush formal gardens have been recreated to Wharton's original design.

Shaker Village

Drive north to **Pittsfield** and then west for 4 miles (6.5km) on Route 20 to the **Hancock Shaker Village ❹** (tel: 413-443-0188; www.hancockshakervillage. org; mid-April–June daily 10am–4pm, July–mid-Nov daily 10am–5pm, mid-Nov–mid-Dec Sat–Sun 10am–5pm), an immaculately preserved reminder of the Shaker religious movement, which peaked in the US in the early 19th century. The buildings, farm, and store selling Shaker reproduction furniture and goods illustrate the sect's devotion to orderly simplicity.

North Adams

From Pittsfield, follow Route 8 for 21 miles (34km) north to **North Adams ❺**, an old industrial town that's undergone something of a revival since the creation of the exciting and enormous **Massachusetts Museum of Contemporary Arts** (MASS MoCA; 87 Marshall Street; tel: 413-662-2111; www.massmoca.org; late June–early Sept daily 10am–6pm Thu–Sat until 7pm, early-Sept–late June Wed–Mon 11am–5pm) that dominates downtown. One of the state's best art museums, MASS MoCA occupies a vast, renovated 19th-century factory complex. Its fine collection of contemporary art, including giant pieces by the likes of Sol LeWitt and Anselm Kiefer, is displayed across 19 light-filled galleries. Within the complex you will also find a performance arts center, presenting a year-round program, and a contemporary art gallery. Dine at the museum's **Grammercy Bistro**, see ❸.

Bridge of Flowers, Shelburne Falls

PIONEER VALLEY

Along the scenic 30-mile (48km) drive east to Greenfield on Route 2, pause at the picturesque village of **Shelburne Falls** ❻, where the unusual **Bridge of Flowers** (www.bridgeofflowersmass.org; free), a 1908 trolley bridge, is now a walkway turned into a delightful garden.

Return to the Pioneer Valley at **Greenfield** and head south, following the Connecticut River. After 3 miles (5km) on Route 5 is **Historic Deerfield** ❼ (The Street; tel: 413-775-7133; www.historic-deerfield.org; mid-Apr–mid-Dec daily 9.30am–4.30pm), a beautifully preserved village commemorating the New England pioneers in 11 museum homes. There are guided walks and demonstrations of traditional pioneer ways of life.

Amherst and Northampton

It's a 15-mile (24km) drive south to the collegiate town of **Amherst** ❽ on Route 5, then 116. The **Emily Dickinson Homestead** (280 Main Street; tel: 413-542-8161; June–Aug Wed–Mon 11am–4pm, Oct–Dec Apr–May Wed–Sun 11am–4pm, Mar Sat–Sun 11am–4pm guided tours only, last tour at 3.30pm) preserves the belongings of the poet who lived in the town throughout her life (1830–86). Nearby is **The Black Sheep**, see ❹.

Finish up in the nearby town of **Northampton** ❾, home of **Smith College** (www.smith.edu), a liberal arts institution for women. Many accomplished women, from Sylvia Plath to Gloria Steinem, studied here.

From Northampton back to Springfield it is 22 miles (35km) down I-91.

Food and drink

❶ NADIM'S DOWNTOWN MEDITERRANEAN RESTAURANT

1390 Main Street, Springfield; tel: 413-737-7373; Mon–Thu 11am–10pm, Fri until 11pm, Sat 3–11pm, Sun 2–8pm; $$
Find Middle Eastern favorites here.

❷ HAVEN CAFÉ AND BAKERY

8 Franklin Street, Lenox; tel: 413-637-8948; Mon–Fri 7.30am–3pm, Sat–Sun 8am–3pm; $–$$
A stylish self-serve operation, with a tempting range of baked goods and breakfast dishes.

❸ GRAMMERCY BISTRO

87 Marshall Street, North Adams; tel: 413-663-5300; www.gramercybistro.com; Wed–Mon 5–9pm, Fri–Sat until 10pm; $$
Overlooking MASS MoCA's main courtyard and upside-down trees, this bistro applies a farm-to-table approach to its international fare.

❹ THE BLACK SHEEP

79 Main Street, Amherst; tel: 413-253-3442; www.blacksheepdeli.com; daily 7am–6pm; $
Hang with the students at this appealingly rustic deli, with creative sandwiches, great drinks, and irresistible baked goods.

Benefit Street

PROVIDENCE

A walk around Rhode Island's handsome capital, which has outstanding 18th- and 19th-century architecture, an excitingly rejuvenated downtown, and a vibrant, arty scene thanks to its prestigious universities and colleges.

DISTANCE: 4 miles (6.5km)
TIME: A full day
START: State House
END: Prospect Terrace
POINTS TO NOTE: Providence is an easy day trip from Boston (51 miles/82km southwest); there is parking beside the Amtrak station.

STATE HOUSE

The white marble dome of **Rhode Island State House 1** (Smith Street; tel: 401-222-3983; www. rilin.state.ri.us; Mon–Fri 8.30am–4.30pm, reserve ahead for morning tours; free) dominates Constitution Hill. Inside, you will find the 1663 charter in which Charles II created the Colony of Rhode Island and Providence Plantations – still the state's official name.

Head south down Francis Street past Providence Place Mall; to the left is **Waterplace Park 2**, an Italian-inspired piazza beside the river; come here from April to October to enjoy the night-time **WaterFire** (www.waterfire.org) displays.

DOWNTOWN

Cross the river and proceed to **Kennedy Plaza**, from where buses to Boston and

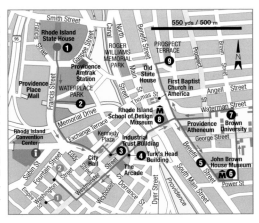

WaterFire display   *Rhode Island State House*

Newport depart. Nearby are many grand edifices, including the Art Deco **Industrial Trust Building** ❸; the **Turk's Head Building** ❹ (1 Turk's Head Place), a 1913 landmark; and the handsome Greek Revival **Arcade** (1828; 65 Weybosset Street), the nation's first indoor shopping mall.

One side of the Arcade is on **Westminster Street**, which exemplifies Downtown's revival with trendy boutiques and eateries, including **Small Point Café**, see ❶, or try **Birch**, see ❷, around the corner on Washington Street.

BENEFIT STREET

Walk back along Westminster Street and cross the river to explore **Benefit Street** ❺, along and around which are more than 200 restored 18th- and 19th-century buildings. Recommended 90-minute walking tours of the area depart from the John Brown House Museum at 10am, Mon–Tue Thu–Sat, mid-May–Oct (see www.rihs.org).

Continue south along Benefit Street and turn left into Power Street to reach the home described by John Quincy Adams as 'the most magnificent and elegant private mansion that I have ever seen on this continent.' Judge for yourself on a tour around the **John Brown House Museum** ❻ (No. 52; tel: 401-331-8575; www.rihs.org; Apr–Nov Tue–Fri 1–4pm, Sat–Sun 10am–4pm) packed with period furniture, paintings, and porcelain.

Turn left onto Brown Street and proceed towards the campus of **Brown University** ❼ (College Hill; http://brown.edu). To the east is the studenty, commercial strip of Thayer Street.

Return to Benefit Street to explore the fantastic **Rhode Island School of Design Museum** ❽ (No. 224; tel: 401-454-6500; www.risdmuseum.org; Tue–Sun 10am–5pm). Among its collection of over 84,000 artworks are fragments from Pompeii, Yemeni tribal dresses and paintings by Picasso and Monet.

Pass behind the **First Baptist Church in America** (www.fbcia.org; Mon–Fri 10am–3pm), established in 1638, and continue to South Court Street. Climb the hill to **Prospect Terrace** ❾ park (Congdon Street), presided over by a statue of Roger Williams, Providence's founder.

Food and drink

❶ SMALL POINT CAFÉ

230 Westminster Street; tel: 401-228-6999; www.smallpointcafe.com; Mon–Fri 7am–7.30pm, Sat 7.30am–7.30pm, Sun 8am–7.30pm; $

Eco-conscious hipster café-bar dishes out sandwiches and salads of organic produce.

❷ BIRCH

200 Washington Street; tel: 401-272-3105; www.birchrestaurant.com; Thu–Mon 5–10pm; $$$

'Modern American' cuisine incorporating top-grade seasonal New England ingredients is served at this elegant restaurant.

The Breakers in winter

NEWPORT

*Stacked with gilded Great Gatsby-esque mansions that their
19th-century millionaire owners referred to as 'summer cottages,'
Newport commands a stunning position on Rhode Island's coast.*

DISTANCE: 3 miles (5km)
TIME: A full day
START: Gateway Visitor Center
END: Marble House
POINTS TO NOTE: This tour can be
combined with that of Providence and a
frequent Ripta bus service (1 hour; www.
ripta.com) links the two. If driving, park at
the Gateway Visitor Center, where you will
also find Newport's Visitor Information
Center (23 America's Cup Avenue; tel:
800-326-6030; www.discovernewport.
org; daily 9am–5pm).

Food and drink

1 BLACK PEARL
Bannister's Wharf; tel: 401-846-5264;
www.blackpearlnewport.com; mid-Feb–
Dec, daily 11.30am–10pm; $$
Popular with the yachting set, this
harborside place is very reliable and offers
a range of dishes from seafood snacks and
sandwiches to grilled meats and fish.

DOWNTOWN

Begin at the **Gateway Visitor Center**,
then walk south along America's Cup
Avenue to the **Museum of Newport His-
tory ❶** (127 Thames Street; tel: 401-
841-8770; http://newporthistory.org;
daily 10am–5pm; donation), on the left
in the 1762 Brick Market building. Follow
Touro Street to No. 85 to find the **Touro
Synagogue ❷** (tel: 401-847-4794;
www.tourosynagogue.org; tours Sun–Fri
except Jewish holidays). Built in 1763,
it is the nation's oldest Jewish house of
worship. Walk south down Spring Street
to Queen Anne Square, home to the
white clapboard 1725–6 **Trinity Episco-
pal Church ❸** (tel: 401-846-0660; www.
trinitynewport.org), said to be based on
the designs of Sir Christopher Wren.
Walk a block west to Newport Harbor to
lunch at the **Black Pearl**, see ❶.

BELLEVUE AVENUE

Many of Newport's attractions line the
thoroughfare of **Bellevue Avenue**. The
1862 **Newport Art Museum ❹** (No. 76;

Trinity Episcopal Church

tel: 401-848-8200; www.newportart museum.org; Tue–Sat 10am–4pm, Sun noon–4pm) has works by George Innes, Winslow Homer, and regional artists.

Housed in the Newport Casino is the **International Tennis Hall of Fame ❺** (No. 194; tel: 401-849-3990; www. tennisfame.com; daily 10am–5pm, July until 6pm). Despite the building's name, it never had anything to do with gambling, but was America's most exclusive country club when it opened in 1880 and hosted the first US National Tennis Championships the following year.

THE MANSIONS

If you plan to tour several mansions, the **Preservation Society of Newport ❻** (242 Bellevue Avenue; tel: 401-847-1000; http://newportmansions.org) sells tickets for admission to up to 10 properties and offers tours; check their website, as hours at the properties vary greatly. The following are recommended.

Coal-rich Edward Julius Berwind commissioned **The Elms ❼** (367 Bellevue Avenue), based on Château d'Asnières near Paris. It borrows from a range of styles, including Chinese, Venetian, and Louis XIV, and is surrounded by gorgeous gardens. Sign up for the 'behind the scenes' tour to see the mansion from the servants' point of view.

An opulent Italian Renaissance palace, completed in 1895 for Cornelius Vanderbilt II, **The Breakers ❽** (44 Ochre Point) is considered the most magnificent of the Newport cottages, with extravagant rooms. The **Marble House ❾** (596 Bellevue Avenue), however, built in 1892 for William K. Vanderbilt and styled after the Grand and Petit Trianons of Versailles, upstages The Breakers for ostentation.

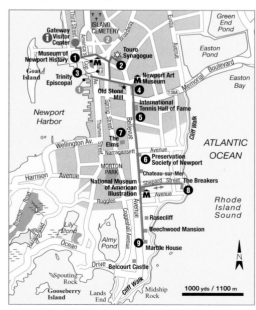

Students make their way to Yale University

CONNECTICUT COAST

Visit pirate islands, ride a steam train, and sail a riverboat down the Connecticut River on this road trip shadowing the Long Island Sound from venerable Yale University to the old port of Mystic.

DISTANCE: 86.5 miles (139km)
TIME: Two days
START: New Haven
END: Mystic
POINTS TO NOTE: Note that Yale's museums are closed on Monday. From Mystic, hop onto I-95 for 50 miles (81km) to reach Providence or turn off after 19 miles (31km) onto Route 138 for Newport. It is 86 miles (138km) via Hartford to Springfield. New Haven and Mystic are also connected with Boston by Amtrak's Northeast Regional line.

This drive from New Haven – home of Ivy League university Yale – to the old whaling port turned tourist town of Mystic, reveals the multifaceted layers of Connecticut's coast, where historic villages of traditional inns and antiques shops lie alongside working naval towns.

NEW HAVEN AND YALE

Settled by Puritans in 1638, **New Haven ❶** was at first a seafaring community but later embraced industry and pioneered such inventions as the meat grinder, the corkscrew, and the steamboat. Today, it is known as the home of prestigious **Yale University**. Founded in 1701 and named after its benefactor, Elihu Yale, the US's third-oldest university is *alma mater* to many presidents, including Bill Clinton and both Bushes.

Park close to **New Haven Green**, the town's center, and walk to the **Yale University Visitor Center** (149 Elm Street; tel: 203-432-2300; http://visitorcenter.

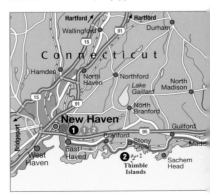

Five Mile Point   Charles W. Morgan at Mystic Seaport Museum

yale.edu; Mon–Fri 9am–4.30pm, Sat–Sun 11am–4pm; free) on the green's north side. Pick up a map or join one of the 95-minute **campus tours** (Mon–Fri 10.30am and 2pm, Sat–Sun 1.30pm).

A classic example of the Ivy League Gothic Revival style of the early 20th century, the campus's attractions include the **University Art Gallery** (111 Chapel Street; tel: 203-432-0600; Tue–Fri 10am–5pm, Thu until 8pm Sept–June, Sat–Sun 11am–5pm; free), with a rich collection of early American decorative and contemporary fine art, and the excellent **Yale Center for British Art** (1080 Chapel Street; tel: 203-432-2800; Tue–Sat 10am–5pm, Sun noon–5pm; free), which boasts the largest collection of British art outside the UK, with works by Turner and Constable.

Take a break at either **Louis' Lunch**, see ❶, or **Da Legna**, see ❷.

THIMBLE ISLANDS

Head east on routes 1 and 146 for 14 miles (22.5km) to the tiny seaside village of **Stony Creek**, embarkation point for a 45-minute boat trip to the **Thimble Islands** ❷ (tel: 203-488-8905; www.thimbleislandcruise.com; May and Sept Fri–Sun, June–Aug Wed–Mon, Oct Sat–Sun, check website for times), 354 rugged outcrops peppered with summer homes.

Hammonasset Beach ❸, 12 miles (19km) farther along routes 146 and 1, is Connecticut's largest waterfront state park. It occupies an entire peninsula, with ample room for swimming, fishing, hiking, and camping (tel: 203-245-2785).

ESSEX

Overlooking the Connecticut River, the genteel town of **Essex** ❹, 17 miles (10.5km) farther east (via Route 1 and,

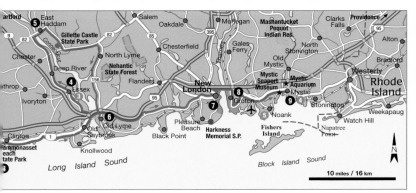

Connecticut River Museum

for a short way, north along Route 9) typifies upscale Yankeedom. Check out the restored 18th-century homes and riverfront dotted with sailboats. Stroll down to the wharfside **Connecticut River Museum** (67 Main Street; tel: 860-767-8269; www.ctrivermuseum.org; Tue–Sun 10am–5pm), which has a working model of the world's first submarine, a design of Yale student David Bushnell in 1776. Grab a bite at **Marley's Café**, see ③.

EAST HADDAM

Ditch the car for an excursion on the **Essex Steam Train and Riverboat** (1 Railroad Avenue; tel: 860-767-0103 or 800-377-3987; www.essexsteamtrain. com) to **East Haddam** ❺. The train, drawn by a 1926 locomotive, clatters north to Deep River Landing, where you change to the riverboat; the entire round trip takes about 2.5 hours.

In East Haddam visit the **Goodspeed Opera House** (6 Main Street; tel: 860-873-8668; www.goodspeed.org), a riverside theatre dating from 1876. A 4-mile (6.5km) drive south is **Gillette Castle State Park** (67 River Road; tel: 860-526-2336; daily 8am–dusk; free), home to an imposing stone 'castle,' (late May–early Sept daily 10am–4.30pm), built in 1914 by eccentric actor William Gillette.

OLD LYME

For a more evocative view of the region's golden past, drive south from East Haddam on routes 82 and 156, which pass through the peaceful countryside that borders Connecticut's west shore. Pause in **Old Lyme** ❻ to visit the **Florence Griswold Museum** (96 Lyme Street; tel: 860-434-5542; www. florencegriswoldmuseum.org; Tue–Sat 10am–5pm, Sun 1–5pm), which has a renowned collection of American Impressionist paintings and recalls the village's heyday as an artists' colony at the start of the 20th century.

NEW LONDON AND GROTON

In the old whaling port of **New London** ❼, 15 miles (24km) east of Old Lyme at the mouth of the Thames River, you will find the **US Coast Guard Academy** (31 Mohegan Avenue; www.cga.edu; free), where the magnificent sailing vessel *Eagle* (tours when in port; tel: 860-444-8444) is used for training coast-guard cadets.

Groton ❽, on the other side of the Thames, is home to the **US Navy Submarine Force Museum** (1 Crystal Lake Road; tel: 860-694-3174; www.ussnautil us.org; May–Oct Wed–Mon 9am–5pm, Nov–Apr Wed–Mon 9am–4pm; free), where you can peek inside the *Nautilus*, the USA's first nuclear submarine.

MYSTIC

With its picture-perfect harbour, **Mystic** ❾, 6 miles (10km) east of Groton, is one of the principal tourist draws of the state's coast.

Essex Steam Train

At the mouth of the Mystic River is the **Mystic Seaport Museum** (75 Greenmanville Avenue; tel: 860-572-5315; www.mysticseaport.org; late Mar–late Oct daily 9am–5pm, late Oct–late Nov daily 10am–4pm, late-Nov–Dec Thu–Sun 10am–4pm), a living history museum spread across 17 acres (7ha), where you will find early 19th-century wharves, stores, and houses. Costumed actors demonstrate crafts and cooking techniques. The collection of 500 vessels includes the whaling ship *Charles W. Morgan* and a *Amistad* slave ship replica.

Mystic offers dozens of dining choices; try **Mystic Pizza**, see ❹ or drive 1.5 miles (2.5km) to **Noank** for **Abbott's Lobster in the Rough**, see ❺.

Out of town near I-95, the **Mystic Aquarium** (55 Coogan Boulevard; tel: 860-572-5955; www.mysticaquarium.org; daily Mar–Oct 9am–5pm, Nov 9am–4pm, Dec–Feb 10am–4pm) numbers seals, sea lions, and beluga whales among its 12,000 fish, invertebrates, and marine mammals. It is also the home of the high-tech Institute for Exploration, with a simulated deep-sea dive

Food and drink

❶ LOUIS' LUNCH
261–263 Crown Street, New Haven; tel: 203-562-5507; www.louislunch.com; Tue–Wed 11am–3.45pm, Thu–Sat noon–2am; $
Devour flame-grilled patties on white toast and strictly no ketchup at this Yale institution.

❷ DA LEGNA
858 State Street, New Haven; tel: 203-495-9999; http://dalegna.com; Mon–Wed 11am–11pm, Thu–Sat 11am–midnight, Sun 9am–11pm; $$
Try some of Connecticut's (and some say the world's) best pizza bakes from the brick wood-fired ovens of this down-home Italian joint sprinkled with industrial chic.

❸ MARLEY'S CAFÉ
11 Ferry Street, Essex; tel: 860-853-0133; late May–early Sept Wed–Mon 7.30am–2pm, July–Oct Fri–Sun 6–9pm; $$
This convivial café, with a view of Essex's marina, serves sandwiches, salads, and seafood dishes, often with a Jamaican flavor.

❹ MYSTIC PIZZA
56 West Main Street, Mystic; tel: 860-536-3700; www.mysticpizza.com; daily 10am–11pm; $–$$
A homely pizza joint that inspired the eponymous 1988 movie starring Julia Roberts.

❺ ABBOT'S LOBSTER IN THE ROUGH
117 Pearl Street, Noank; tel: 860-536-7719; http://abbottslobster.com; late-May–early-Sept daily 11.30am–9pm, early May and mid-Sept–mid Oct Fri–Sun 11.30am–7pm; $$
Head to the waterfront to enjoy fresh lobster and other seafood dishes alfresco. BYOB.

Newfane courthouse

THE GREEN MOUNTAINS

This two-day drive along the VT 100, the meandering backbone of Vermont, takes you straight to the leafy heart of this laid-back state and ends at the sophisticated town of Woodstock, close to the premier ski resort of Killington.

DISTANCE: 83 miles (134km)
TIME: Two days
START: Brattleboro
END: Woodstock
POINTS TO NOTE: This route can connect with the Berkshires to the south. You can join the Lake Champlain Valley tour by driving 46 miles (74km) north from Woodstock to Brandon along Route 7. Or head east for 70 miles (113km) via Route 4 to Meredith in the Lakes Region of New Hampshire.

Nearly every image conjured by the name 'Vermont' comes to life along this leisurely itinerary, ticking off the picturesque little villages and arty towns that line the southern half of scenic Route 100. You will see rolling dairy farms dotted with black-and-white cows and the tree-covered slopes of the Green Mountains. The spectacular fall colors are world-famous.

BRATTLEBORO

With a granola-and-sandals bohemian atmosphere, **Brattleboro** ❶, on the banks of the Connecticut River, will provide a relaxed start to your trip. Near the site of Vermont's first permanent settlement and founded in 1724, Brattleboro had been a busy manufacturing center in the 19th century but was on the downturn by the 20th century. Concerned local artists and activists came to the rescue, founding the Brattleboro Arts Initiative (www.brattleboroarts.org) in 1998.

Among the initiative's successes has been its taking over of the stylish Art Deco **Latchis Memorial Building** (50 Main Street), which includes a hotel (see page 103) and adjacent cinema, now closed. Across the way, at 10 Vernon Street, the **Brattleboro Museum and Art Center** (tel: 802-257-0124; www.brattleboromuseum.org; Wed–Mon 11am–5pm) recounts local history, and hosts changing art exhibitions as well as occasional music events.

Head 7 miles (11km) north to Putney, via I-91, for a fine feed at **Curtis' All American Barbecue Pit**, see ❶.

Vermont in fall   _A covered Vermont bridge_

NEWFANE TO WESTON

For the 50-mile (80km) drive to Weston, first follow Route 30 along the West River valley, heading north at Rawsonville onto Route 100. En route you will pass through a series of pretty Vermont settlements centered on village greens. **Newfane ❷** (www.newfanevt.com) is one of the best, with its 1825 Greek Revival courthouse, whitewashed churches, and cluster of antiques shops. The town hosts a **flea market** (May–Oct Sun from 6am) on Route 30.

Scott Bridge

About 6 miles (10km) north of Newfane, pause to inspect the **Scott Bridge ❸**. Built in 1870, and now open only to pedestrians, the 275ft (85m) covered structure is Vermont's longest wooden bridge. You will spot several such covered bridges along this route and elsewhere in New England; their design helps protect the bridges' frames from the elements.

Stratton Mountain

Routes 30 and 100 join at East Jamaica, continuing together for 8 miles (13km) along the east boundary of the **Green Mountain National Forest** (www.fs.usda.gov). You are now entering the heart of south Vermont's ski country, with the slopes of **Stratton Mountain** looming to the left. For panoramic vistas during foliage season, go west for 4 miles (6.5km) on Route 30 from Rawsonville to ride the **Stratton Gondola**

❹ (Route 1; tel: 802-297-2200; www.stratton.com; see website for times, foliage season late Sept–mid-Oct) to the peak. Otherwise, keep heading north along Route 100. A short way on is the pretty village of **South Londonderry**, home of **SoLo Farm & Table**, see ❷.

WESTON

The next stop along Route 100 is pristine **Weston ❺**, where the ample town green is circled by homes dating back to the 1790s. On the green, the **Weston Playhouse** (tel: 802-824-5288; www.westonplayhouse.org; late June–early

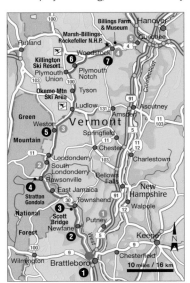

Dairy cows at Billings Farm

Sept) has hosted summer theater productions for over 60 years.

Vermont Country Store

Most visitors are drawn to Weston by the celebrated **Vermont Country Store** (657 Main Street; tel: 802-824-3184; www. vermontcountrystore.com; daily 9am–5.30pm), a throwback to old-time, small-town emporia. With a potbellied stove and a penny-candy counter, the store has grown into an omnium-gatherum of all sorts of practical items. When it comes to lunch, the store's **Bryant House**, see ❸, is a good bet.

PLYMOUTH NOTCH HISTORIC DISTRICT

Calvin Coolidge was one of two US presidents born in Vermont (the other was Chester A. Arthur). Coolidge's ancestral village of **Plymouth Notch** ❻, located in

the hills 32 miles (51km) north of Weston via routes 100 and 100A, is preserved as the **Plymouth Notch Historic District** (tel: 802-672-3773; http://historicsites. vermont.gov; late May–mid-Oct daily 9.30am–5pm) You can see Coolidge's father's general store, the family's cheese company, and the house in which he took the oath of office on August 2, 1923, when, as vice-president, he learned of President Harding's death. A dyed-in-the-wool conservative Yankee, Coolidge would no doubt approve if he could see how little Plymouth Notch has changed.

WOODSTOCK

It is another Vermont altogether at **Woodstock** ❼, 17 miles (27km) east of Plymouth Notch via routes 100A and 4. The roaring Ottauquechee River here once powered wool mills, and it was on a nearby hillside in 1934 that the state's first ski tow presaged Vermont's modern tourist economy. Also instrumental in Woodstock's transformation was the late Laurance Rockefeller's acquisition of the **Woodstock Inn** (see page 104), which he turned into one of Vermont's plushest hostelries.

Woodstock's town center, a sophisticated place of galleries, boutiques, and cafés, is surrounded by block after block of handsomely restored Federal and Greek Revival homes. For lunch, try **Mon Vert Cafe**, see ❹, or head 7 miles (11km) out of town to **Simon Pearce**, see ❺, in **Quechee**.

Killington

Some of New England's best skiing is to be found at Killington (tel: 1-800-621-6867; www.killington.com), 20 miles (32km) west of Woodstock. Offering 200 runs over seven mountains and a drop of over 3,000ft (900m), this is Vermont's premier ski resort, with a season that runs from late November to late May. When the snow melts, it becomes a destination for mountain bikers, who coast down some 45 miles (72km) of trails.

Skiing at Killington   *Woodstock Inn*

Marsh-Billings-Rockefeller National Historical Park

Well worth exploring are the mansion and grounds at **Marsh-Billings-Rockefeller National Historical Park** (tel: 802-457-3368; www.nps.gov/mabi; late May–Oct daily 10am–5pm; grounds free, mansion charge), just out of town on Route 12. This 500-acre (200ha) woodland tract, threaded with hiking trails and carriage roads, honors George Perkins Marsh, a 19th-century Woodstock native and early conservationist, who advised the property's owner, the railroad magnate and gentleman farmer Frederick Billings.

On the other side of Route 12 is the **Billings Farm and Museum** (tel: 802-457-2355; www.billingsfarm.org; Apr–late Oct daily 10am–5pm, Nov–Feb Sat–Sun 10am–4pm), a working model farm since Billings's day. In addition to its prize dairy herd, the farm features an excellent collection of antique farm implements and local-history exhibits..

Food and drink

① CURTIS' ALL AMERICAN BAR-BE-CUE PIT

7 Putney Landing Road, Putney; tel: 802-387-5474; Wed–Sun 10am–dusk; $
Curtis' barbecued pork ribs and chicken with sides are delicious, even though the food comes out of two school buses turned into kitchens.

② SOLO FARM & TABLE

95 Middletown Road, South Londonderry; tel: 802-824-6327; http://solofarmandtable.com; Mon, Thu, Sun 5.30–9pm Fri–Sat until 10pm; $$
Local farmers and growers provide the ingredients for these tuned-up versions of regional dishes with international influences.

③ BRYANT HOUSE

Route 100, Weston; tel: 802-824-6287; mid-June–mid-Sept daily 11am–8pm, mid-Sept–mid June 11am–3.30pm; $$

The old-fashioned home-style cooking served here includes chicken pie with gravy and pancakes that come with a souvenir bottle of local maple syrup.

④ MON VERT CAFE

28 Central Street, Woodstock; tel: 802-457-7143; www.monvertcafe.com; daily 7.30am–5pm; $–$$
One of Woodstock's favorite breakfast and lunch spots dishes up sandwiches, salads, and biscuits and gravy, many using local and organic ingredients.

⑤ SIMON PEARCE RESTAURANT

1760 Quechee Main Street, Quechee; tel: 802-295-4600; www.simonpearce.com; Mon–Sat 11.30am–2.45pm, 5.30–9pm, Sun from 10:30am; $
One of Vermont's most romantic restaurants serves elegant American comfort food in an old mill perched above the Ottauquechee River waterfall.

Stately Burlington architecture

BURLINGTON AND LAKE CHAMPLAIN VALLEY

On the east shore of beautiful Lake Champlain is Burlington, Vermont's largest and most diverse city. From here, this driving tour rambles through the broad Champlain valley and lofty passes of the Green Mountains.

DISTANCE: 130 miles (209km) round trip
TIME: Two days
START/END: Burlington
POINTS TO NOTE: If you are connecting from the Green Mountains route, begin at Brandon. Amtrak's Vermonter train stops in Essex Junction, 5 miles (8km) east of Burlington, and Burlington International Airport (www.btv.aero) is 3 miles (5km) east. Meredith, in the Lakes Region of New Hampshire, is 147 miles (237km) southeast via I-89 and Route 4.

BURLINGTON

Vermont's 'Queen City,' **Burlington** ❶ enjoys a hillside location facing the broadest part of Lake Champlain. Orientate yourself at the **Waterfront Park** and adjacent **ECHO Lake Aquarium & Science Center** (1 College Street; tel: 877-324-6386; www.echovermont.org; daily 10am–5pm). Here, exhibits explain the natural history of the 125-mile (200km) long lake and explore the mystery of

Champ, its mythical aquatic monster. Nearby, grab a crêpe at **Skinny Pancake**, see ❶.

Ferries and boats

From the King Street landing, just south of the park, car and passenger ferries (tel: 802-864-9804; www.ferries.com) make the one-hour crossing to Port Kent, New York. Alternatively, take a trip on the cruise ship **Spirit of Ethan Allen II** (Burlington Community Boathouse; tel: 802-862-8300; www.soea.com) or the **Friend Ship sloop** (tel: 802-825-7245; www.whistlingman.com), or rent a kayak or canoe from **Community Sailing Center** (234 Penny Lane; tel: 802-864-2499; http://communitysailingcenter.org).

Downtown

Burlington's lively downtown is dominated by pedestrianised Church Street, with its bistros, boutiques, and craft galleries such as the **Vermont Craft Center Frog Hollow** (No. 85; www.froghollow.org), exhibiting works by Vermont artisans. For a meal, stop in at **Penny Cluse Café**, see ❷.

Lake Champlain   *The Ticonderoga at the Shelburne Museum*

University of Vermont Campus

The hilltop **University of Vermont** (UVM; www.uvm.edu) campus is worth exploring. Along University Place stand an array of college buildings, including the 1825 **Old Mill** (the cornerstone was laid by the Marquis de Lafayette), and the Romanesque, 1886 **Billings Student Center**.

Around the corner is the **Fleming Museum** (61 Colchester Avenue; tel: 802-656-0750; www.uvm.edu/~fleming; check website for hours), with an excellent collection of European and American art, plus ethnographic exhibits from around the world.

SHELBURNE

Head south out of Burlington on Route 7 for 10 miles (16km) to **Shelburne ❷**, where the **Shelburne Museum** (tel: 802-985-3346; www.shelburnemuseum.org; May–Dec daily 10am–5pm, Jan–Apr Wed–Sun 10am–5pm,) holds one of the nation's premier collections of Americana. Largely the legacy of heiress Electra Havemeyer Webb, the vast collection includes folk art, tools, and horse-drawn vehicles, set among 39 buildings on 45 landscaped acres (18ha). Don't miss the *Ticonderoga*, a 1906 Lake Champlain passenger steamer.

Shelburne Farms

Set aside a good half-day to explore **Shelburne Farms** (1611 Harbor Road; tel: 802-985-8686; www.shelburnefarms.org; mid-May–mid-Oct 10am–4pm, grounds open year-round), the Webbs' country estate and model

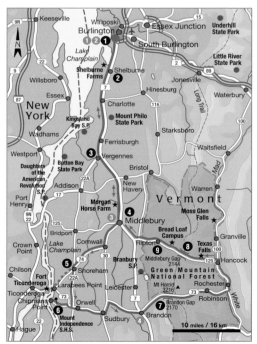

A Vermont round barn at the Shelburne Museum

farm. You can view cheesemaking and other enterprises as well as explore the beautiful lakeside grounds. Children will love encountering the various farmyard animals. The 1880s Farm and Breeding Barns are magnificent, and you can stay at Dr William Seward and Lila Vanderbilt Webb's grand home, now the **Inn at Shelburne Farms** (see page 104).

VERGENNES

The small town of **Vergennes** ❸, 14 miles (23km) south of Shelburne, has delightful Victorian architecture as well as the **Lake Champlain Maritime Museum** (4472 Basin Harbor Road; tel: 802-475-2022; www.lcmm.org; late May–mid-Oct daily 10am–5pm). The exhibits, including a collection of antique watercraft and a replica of the *Philadelphia*, a Revolutionary War gunboat, relate the history of navigation on the lake.

MIDDLEBURY

Straddling the gushing waters of Otter's Creek is the attractive college town of **Middlebury** ❹, 13 miles (21km) farther south via Route 7. On its west edge, the campus of Middlebury College, a 200-year-old liberal arts institution, features an interesting **Museum of Art** (Route 30; tel: 802-443-5007; http://museum.middlebury.edu; Tue–Fri 10am–5pm, Sat–Sun noon–5pm, closed late Aug and most Dec; free), with Asian and Western works.

Just off the town green is the white-washed 1809 **Congregational Church**, its steeple rising 135ft (40m) in four tiers. Also downtown, in an 1829 quarry magnate's house, is the **Henry Sheldon Museum of Vermont History** (1 Park Street; tel: 802-388-2117; www.henrysheldonmuseum.org; Tue–Sat 10am–5pm, late May–mid Oct also Sun 1–5), with a collection of 18th- and 19th-century Vermontiana. For something to eat, try **American Flatbread**, see ❸.

CHIPMAN'S PORT

Traveling through some of Vermont's lushest dairy lands, head southwest via Routes 30 and 74 for 13 miles (21km) to **Shoreham** ❺, famous for its apple crop and fresh-pressed cider. Continue south along Route 22A to **Orwell**, turn right and head west to **Chipman's Point** and **Mount Independence State Historic Site** ❻ (tel: 802-948-2000; http://historicsites.vermont.gov; grounds daily, Visitor Center late May–mid-Oct daily 9.30am–5pm). This attraction concentrates on an American fort that commanded the lake in the battle against the British during the War of Independence. Various exhibits relate the story.

GREEN MOUNTAIN NATIONAL FOREST

Retrace your route back to Orwell and continue on Route 73 through to **Brandon**. The entire core of the town (more

Kayaking, Lake Champlain

At the wheel at the Vergennes Maritime Museum

than 200 buildings) is listed on the National Register of Historic Places. Dine at **Café Provence**, see ❹.

From Brandon, Route 73 climbs into the heart of the north portion of the **Green Mountain National Forest** (see page 75). The highest point, at 2,170ft (661m), along the winding 17-mile (27km) road to Route 100 is at **Brandon Gap** ❼. The **Long Trail** (www.greenmountain-club.org), Vermont's 'Footpath through the Wilderness,' crosses the road here and affords hiking access to the 3,216ft (980m) summit of **Mount Horrid**.

Middlebury Gap and Ripton

Follow Route 100 north for 5 miles (8km) north to **Hancock**, then turn left for the 21-mile (34km) drive toward Middlebury on Route 125. Heading west, follow a steep route through rugged terrain that peaks at the 2,144ft (653m) **Middlebury Gap** ❽. Halfway between Hancock and the gap is a right-hand turnoff for **Texas Falls**, a beautiful cascade.

Continuing across the gap, Route 125 descends into **Ripton** ❾, the one-time summer home of Robert Frost. A couple of miles before arriving in this hamlet, you will pass through the idyllic **Bread Loaf Campus** of Middlebury College, an unmissable collection of mustard-yellow-painted buildings with emerald-green trims. Also nearby is the **Robert Frost Wayside Area**, good for picnics; across the way, a mile (1.5km) long trail through the forest is lined with quotes from the poet's works.

After Ripton, Route 125 joins with Route 7 to bring you back to Middlebury and on to Burlington.

Food and drink

❶ SKINNY PANCAKE

60 Lake Street, Burlington; tel: 802-540-0188; www.skinnypancake.com; Sun–Wed 8am–10pm, Thu–Sat 8am–11pm; $
Fill up on all kinds of crêpes, sweet and savory, with a view of Lake Champlain. In the evenings there is live music and fondue.

❷ PENNY CLUSE CAFÉ

169 Cherry Street, Burlington; tel: 802-651-8834; www.pennycluse.com; Mon–Fri 6.45am–3pm, Sat–Sun 8am–3pm; $
Try gingerbread pancakes at this super-popular café (expect to wait in line) or the gut-busting breakfast and lunch dishes.

❸ AMERICAN FLATBREAD

137 Maple Street, Middlebury; tel: 802-388-3300; http://americanflatbread.com; Tue–Sat 5–9pm; $$
The best pizzas in Vermont are baked in the wood-fired, clay ovens of this local franchise.

❹ CAFÉ PROVENCE

11 Center Street, Brandon; tel: 802-247-9997; www.cafeprovencevt.com; Mon–Fri 11.30am–9pm, Sat–Sun from 9am; $$
French chef Robert has locals lapping up his American diner classics, using locally grown, seasonally available produce.

Morning mist on Lake Winnipesaukee

THE LAKES REGION

Shimmering at New Hampshire's heart is Lake Winnipesaukee. Dotted with over 300 islands and surrounded by forested hills, it is home to long-established vacation towns, including Wolfeboro and Weirs Beach. There are also quieter villages and smaller lakes to be enjoyed on this circular route.

DISTANCE: 74 miles (119km)
TIME: One to two days
START/END: Wolfeboro
POINTS TO NOTE: Conway is 36 miles (58km) north; Portsmouth is 48 miles (77km) southeast.

LAKE WINNIPESAUKEE

Squashed between Lake Wentworth and **Lake Winnipesaukee**, the state's largest body of water, is **Wolfeboro ❶**. John Wentworth, a New Hampshire governor, built a summer retreat here in 1769 – hence Wolfeboro's claim to be 'America's oldest summer resort.' A pleasant place for a meal is **Garwoods**, see ❶.

Weirs Beach

Follow Route 28 south for 10 miles (16km) to the tiny town of **Alton Bay**, then head north along Route 11 to family-friendly **Weirs Beach ❷**. Stacked with game arcades such as the enormous **Funspot** (www.funspotnh. com), this resort town verges on the tacky but will be a hit with kids. You can also board the **M/S Mount Washington** (tel: 603-366-5531; www.cruisenh.com; 2.5-hour cruise), an elegant 1888 steamship (now diesel) that has served as a pleas-

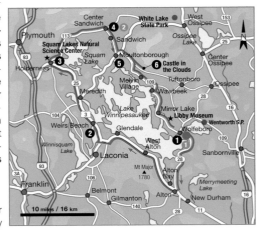

Castle in the Clouds

ure cruiser here since 1940. There's a nice public beach at Endicott Park.

SQUAM LAKE

Continue north on Route 3 through the arty town of **Meredith** to **Squam Lake ③**. **Holderness** is the main town here and, like Squam Lake itself, its image contrasts sharply with the tourist-oriented west shore of Winnipesaukee. This is the genteel, old-money summer milieu captured in the 1981 film *On Golden Pond*, which was filmed here. The **Squam Lakes Natural Science Center** (tel: 603-968-7194; www.nhnature.org; May–Oct daily 9.30am–5pm) is a 200-acre (80ha) preserve, which features native wildlife in a woodland setting, trails, interactive exhibits, and animal programs.

CENTER SANDWICH

Follow Route 113, as it curves north then east, for 13 miles (21km) to the trim village of **Center Sandwich ④** (www.discoversandwich.com), where the **League of New Hampshire Craftsmen** (www.nhcrafts.org) was launched more than 70 years ago. The league's first store is at 32 Main Street (May–Oct Mon–Sat 10am–5pm, Sun noon–5pm); across the street is the **Corner House Inn**, see ②.

MOULTONBOROUGH

Follow Route 109 south for 4 miles (6km) to **Moultonborough ⑤**, where the **Old Country Store** (1011 Whittier Highway; tel: 603-476-5750; www.nhcountrystore.com; daily 9am–5pm) has been selling necessities since it was built as a stagecoach stop in 1781, and has a small museum of artifacts to prove it.

Three miles (5km) from Moultonborough, off Route 109, is the **Castle in the Clouds ⑥** (Route 171; tel: 603-476-5900; www.castleintheclouds.org; mid-May Sat–Sun 10am–5.30pm, late-May–late-Oct daily). Shoe manufacturer Thomas G. Plant started to build this fantasy homemade of granite in 1911, on a lofty site overlooking the Ossipee Mountains. Return to Route 109 for 17 miles (27km) back to Wolfeboro.

Food and drink

① GARWOODS

6 North Main Street, Wolfeboro; tel: 603-569-7788; www.garwoodsrestaurant.com; daily 11.30am–9pm; $$

A wood-beamed restaurant with a decent selection of food and seating by the lake.

② CORNER HOUSE INN

22 Main Street, Center Sandwich; tel: 603-284-6219; www.cornerhouseinn.com; Mon, Wed–Thu 4.30–9pm, Fri–Sat 4.30–10pm, Sun 11.30am–9pm; $–$$

This former inn and carriage house offers a good-value menu that takes in seafood, flatbread pizzas, and burgers, and includes locally sourced ingredients.

View from Mount Willard

THE WHITE MOUNTAINS

Train enthusiasts and hikers will enjoy this loop drive through New Hampshire's picturesque White Mountains, which includes an ascent of Mount Washington – New England's highest point.

> **DISTANCE:** 109 miles (175km)
> **TIME:** Two days
> **START/END:** Conway
> **POINTS TO NOTE:** This tour can be linked with New Hampshire's Lakes Region. Portland in Maine is 61 miles (98km) southeast.

New Hampshire's White Mountains emerged as a tourist playground in the late 19th-century days of railroad travel and grand hotels, when the uplands provided a cool summer haven. Sections of the original railroad still see tourist trains today, while the 800,000-acre (325,000ha) White Mountain National Forest offers miles of unspoiled vistas and marvelous hiking terrain.

KANCAMAGUS HIGHWAY

Named for a 17th-century Native American chief, the **Kancamagus Highway** ❶ (Route 112) runs 26.5 miles (43km) from just west of **Conway** to Lincoln. Passing through the White Mountain National Forest, the road constitutes one of New England's great scenic experiences, cresting the 2,860ft (872m), elevated **Kancamagus Pass**.

At the Lincoln end you will find the popular ski resort **Loon Mountain** (tel: 603-745-8111; www.loonmtn.com), and on the west side of I-93 in **North Woodstock**, the **Woodstock Inn**, see ❶. Just to the north on Route 3, kids will enjoy the mini theme park **Clark's Trading Post** ❷ (No. 110; tel: 603-745-8913; www.clarkstradingpost.com; mid-May–mid-Oct, hours vary), where attractions include a 30-minute excursion on the White Mountain Central Railroad.

FRANCONIA NOTCH

From North Woodstock head north through the **Franconia Notch** ❸ mountain pass. The state park here contains **The Flume** (tel: 603-745-8391; www.visitnh.gov/flume; May–Oct daily 9am–5pm), an 800ft (245m) glacially carved chasm through which a walkway follows a rushing stream and waterfalls. The round walk takes around an hour.

Dog-sledding at the Mount Washington Resort

Robert Frost (1874–1963) wrote some of his most famous poems at **The Frost Place** (tel: 603-823-5510; www.frostplace.org; late May–June Thu–Sun 1–5pm, July Wed–Mon 1–5pm, Sept–mid-Oct Wed–Mon 10am–5pm). There's an educational center for poetry and the arts, as well as a nature trail. To get there, drive 1 mile (1.5km) south of Franconia on Route 116. Turn left on Bickford Hill Road and left again on Ridge Road.

Cannon Mountain Tramway

Farther up I-93, the **Cannon Mountain Aerial Tramway** (tel: 603-823-8800;

www.cannonmt.com; late May–mid-Oct and Dec–mid-Apr daily 8.30am–5pm) serves the Cannon Mountain ski area, providing sweeping views of the ranges. Near the cable-car base, the **New England Ski Museum** (tel: 603-823-7177; www.skimuseum.org; late-May–early Apr 10am–5pm; free) displays evocative photos and antique equipment.

WHITE MOUNTAINS HIGHWAY

Turn off I-93 onto Route 302, the **White Mountains Highway**, to reach the resort town of **Bethlehem ❹**, popular

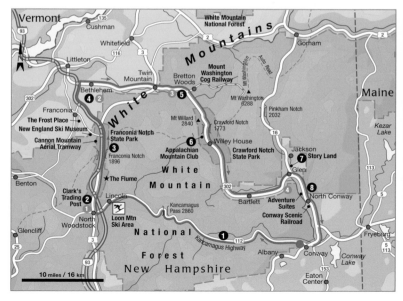

with allergy sufferers, who benefit from its pollen-free environment, and golfers, who enjoy the nearby courses. In the heart of town itself, **Marketplace at WREN** (2011 Main Street; tel: 603-869-3100; www.wrencommunity.org; daily 10am–5pm) showcases the craftwork of over 200 local artisans; next door is **Cold Mountain Café**, see ❷.

Bretton Woods and Mount Washington Resort

The highway leads up to Crawford Notch, the third mountain pass on this route, passing through the resort area of **Bretton Woods** ❺ on the way. Famous for

being the location of a World War II conference, it is home to the historic **Mount Washington Hotel** (see page 106), the sole survivor of several grand late 19th-century hotels that put the White Mountains on the vacation map. Today the beautifully restored hotel is the focus of the **Omni Mount Washington Resort** (tel: 603-278-1000; www.omnihotels.com), which includes facilities for skiers, golfers, horseback riders, and hikers; drop by for afternoon tea if nothing else.

Reservations are essential for the resort's **Canopy Tour** (tel: 603-278-4947), on which would-be action heroes can spend a thrilling 3.5 hours traversing the mountain tops using 10 ziplines, two sky bridges, and three rappels.

Mount Washington Cog Railway

Next to the resort restaurant, **Fabyan's Station**, see ❸, is the turnoff to the **Mount Washington Cog Railway** (tel: 603-278-5404; www.thecog.com; late Apr–Nov, check website for times), completed in 1869. Coal-fired steam locomotives still haul passengers up gradients so steep they are almost sheer to the 6,300ft (1,900m) peak; the round-trip, including a 20-minute stop at the summit, takes three hours.

At the top is the **Sherman Adams Summit Building** (tel: 603-466-3988; www.mountwashington.org), a fascinating institution that presents a history of weather; the world's highest wind speed of 231mph (372kph) was recorded here in 1936.

Mt Washington Road

There are a couple more ways of reaching the summit of Mount Washington other than on the Cog Railway. One is to hike there – a common route is from Pinkham Notch, the easternmost pass through the White Mountains, 10 miles (16km) north of Glen along Route 16. Alternatively, five miles (8km) farther north is the base station for the Mount Washington Auto Road (tel: 603-466-3988; www.mtwashington autoroad.com; early May–late Oct daily, check website for times), which opened in 1861. The gradients of this 8-mile (13km) toll route to the summit reach 18 degrees. The road is a highway to the clouds and magnificent views when they disperse. If you don't fancy driving up yourself, there are also guided tours.

Mount Washington Cog Railway

Crawford Notch

Farther along the highway, near the crest of **Crawford Notch**, the **Appalachian Mountain Club** ❻ (tel: 617-523-0636; www.outdoors.org) has built a handsome lodge, offering rooms, meals, and dormitory accommodations (see page 106). Guided walks and outdoor gear (loaned for free) are also available here.

TOWARD NORTH CONWAY

Head down the highway, past the town of **Bartlett** and the **White Mountain Cider Company**, see ❹, toward **Glen**. Just to the north, on Route 16, is the theme park **Story Land** ❼ (tel: 603-383-4186; www.storylandnh.com; late May–mid-Oct,

check website for days and times), with 21 family-friendly rides in a storybook setting. Head south to North Conway.

Conway Scenic Railroad

From the row of shops and hotels that line the highway, it is clear that **North Conway** ❽ is the commercial capital of White Mountains tourism. Try to time your arrival to coincide with one of the departures along the **Conway Scenic Railroad** (tel: 603-356-5251; www.conwayscenic.com; May–Dec). Trains leave from a Victorian station across the green in the town center. The railway offers the chance to have lunch or dinner in the Chocorura dining car. It is 6 miles (9.5km) south to Conway.

Food and drink

❶ WOODSTOCK INN
North Woodstock; tel: 603-745-3951; www.woodstockinnnh.com; daily 11.30am–10pm; $$
A super extensive menu and on-site microbrewery are the pluses at this Victorian country inn that incorporates the old Lincoln railway station.

❷ COLD MOUNTAIN CAFÉ
2015 Main Street, Bethlehem; tel: 603-869-2500; www.coldmountaincafe.com; Mon–Sat 11am–3pm 5–9pm; $–$$
A pleasant café and gallery next to the Marketplace at WREN craft shop.

❸ FABYAN'S STATION
Route 302, Bretton Woods; tel: 603-278-2222; www.omnihotels.com; mid-May to mid-Oct, mid-Dec to mid-Apr daily 11.30am–9pm; $$
Fabyan's serves chicken wings, burgers, soups, and salads.

❹ WHITE MOUNTAIN CIDER COMPANY
Route 302, Bartlett; tel: 603-383-9061; www.ciderconh.com; deli daily 7am–5pm, restaurant Sun–Thu 5–9pm Fri–Sat until 10pm; $–$$$
Stop by this deli for cheap coffee, freshly made cider donuts and apple cider, as well as sandwiches. The evening restaurant in a rustic barn provides contemporary gourmet cuisine.

Portsmouth is sited on the Piscataqua River

PORTSMOUTH

History buffs, garden lovers, and foodies will love this meander around Portsmouth, one of New England's oldest settlements, where aspects of four centuries of American life are preserved and celebrated.

DISTANCE: 2 miles (3.25km)
TIME: a full day
START: Strawbery Banke museum
END: John Paul Jones house
POINTS TO NOTE: Most of Portsmouth's sights are only open from June to mid-October. C&J (www.ridecj.com) runs a bus service (1.5 hours) between Boston and Portsmouth's transit centre, off I-95, from where a trolley bus (www.coast bus.org) will take you into town. Portland, Maine, is 52 miles (84km) north via I-95.

Food and drink

❶ GENO'S CHOWDER AND SANDWICH SHOP

177 Mechanic Street; tel: 603-427-2070; www.genoschowder.com; Mon–Sat 11am–4pm; $
This whitewashed, riverside cottage dishes up fish chowder and lobster rolls.

Standing at the mouth of the Piscataqua River, and graced with a superb natural harbor, Portsmouth is the nation's third-oldest English settlement. Much of its 400-year history has been lovingly preserved in the downtown area, peppered with historic houses. Its many delicious dining options also make the compact town a fine destination for gourmets.

STRAWBERRY BANKE

Pull into Hancock Street and park in front of the **Strawbery Banke Museum** ❶ (Marcy Street; tel: 603-433-1100; http://strawberybanke.org; May–Oct daily 10am–5pm). This urban quarter of 42 preserved houses is Portsmouth's highlight. The English named their 1623 colony for the profusion of wild strawberries that greeted them; today, the 10-acre (4ha) living history museum tells the story of the city's oldest neighborhood from 1650 to 1950. Costumed guides and artisans make barrels and pottery, tend the lovely gardens, and keep up lively repartee in such roles as an immigrant Jewish woman from 1919..

Strawbery Banke   *Tugboat in the harbor*

Prescott Park

It is hard to believe that the genteel area of pretty cottages around Strawbery Banke was once Portsmouth's red light district. The efforts of the local Prescott sisters helped clean the area up, and it is for them that the nearby riverside **Prescott Park ❷** is named.

HISTORIC HOUSES

Just south are two of Portsmouth's many historic house museums: **Wentworth-Gardner House** and **Tobias Lear House ❸** (50 Mechanic Street; tel: 603-436-4406; http://wentworthlear.org; late May–mid-Oct Thu–Mon 11am–4pm). In the former, a 1760 structure facing the Piscataqua River, are photographs by Wallace Nutting, a founder of the Colo-

nial Revival movement. Nearby is **Geno's Chowder & Sandwich Shop**, see ❶.

Walk back past Prescott Park and turn left on Daniel Street to view the 1716 **Warner House ❹** (No. 150; tel: 603-436-5909; www.warnerhouse.org; June–mid-Oct Wed–Mon 11am–4pm). This was the first of Portsmouth's many brick houses, and sports a stairwell decorated with an array of early 18th-century murals.

Old warehouses transformed into restaurants and boutiques line Bow Street leading around to Market Street, where you will find the **Moffatt-Ladd House and Garden ❺** (No. 54; tel: 603-436-8221; www.moffattladd.org; tours June–mid-Oct, Mon–Sat 11am–5pm, Sun 1–5pm), a three-story Georgian mansion topped with a captain's walk and graced with English-style terraced gardens.

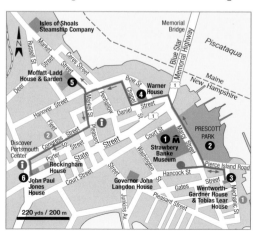

Walk south along Market Street, turn right on Congress Street and left on Middle Street. More pretty gardens front the **John Paul Jones House ❻** (No. 43; tel: 603-436-8420; www.portsmouthhistory.org; late-May–mid-Oct daily 11am–5pm). The Revolutionary War naval hero once rented a room here.

Just on State Street is **Rockingham House**, where the treaty ending the 1905 Russo-Japanese War was signed.

Portland

PORTLAND AND MIDCOAST MAINE

From the arty metropolis of Portland to the upscale sailing town of Camden, this route explores Midcoast Maine, taking in a genteel university town, quaint fishing villages, and the retail delights of Freeport.

DISTANCE: 87 miles (140km)
TIME: Two to three days
START: Portland
END: Camden
POINTS TO NOTE: For more information on Portland, see www.downtown portland.org. Amtrak's Downeaster train service (www.amtrakdowneaster.com) connects Boston with Portland. Castine, start of the Down East Maine tour, is 54 miles (87km) north around the coast.

PORTLAND

There's a gritty urban vibe to **Portland ❶**, Maine's largest city, where you will find revived, 19th-century red-brick and stone warehouses and buildings in the Old Port District, cutting-edge art galleries, and a host of gastronomic delights. The waterfront is an atmospheric place to hang on a warm summer evening.

Portland Museum of Art

Begin at the **Portland Museum of Art ❹** (7 Congress Square; tel: 207-775-6148; www.portlandmuseum.org; Tue–Sun 10am–5pm, Fri until 9pm, mid-May–mid-Oct also Mon 10am–5pm; free), the nucleus around which many small commercial galleries gravitate. Maine's largest public art institution contains a collection that spans three centuries of American art by the likes of Andrew Wyeth, Winslow Homer, and Andy Warhol, as well as works by European masters, such as Renoir, Monet, and Picasso. A highlight is the McLellan House, a beautifully preserved townhouse from 1801.

Wadsworth Longfellow House

From the art museum it's a five-minute walk down Congress Street, past the outstanding restaurant **Five Fifty-Five** (see page 117) to **Wadsworth Longfellow House ❸** (No. 489; tel: 207-774-1822; www.mainehistory.org; May–Oct Mon–Sat 10am–5pm Sun noon–5pm, Nov–Apr Tue–Sat 10am–5pm), childhood home of Portland's most famous literary son. Guided tours are conducted around the 1785 brick house – Portland's oldest such structure – as well as its restored Colonial Revival garden.

Dark Harbor Fishermen (1943) by N.C. Wyeth, at the Portland Museum of Art

Old Port District

Portland owes much of its present-day distinction to the transformation of its dilapidated waterfront district into the **Old Port District ⊖** (roughly bounded by Middle, Union, and Commerical streets). This buzzing neighborhood is packed with crafts shops, boutiques, cafés, and restaurants: try **Duckfat**, see **❶**, at the far end of Middle Street for lunch.

Return toward the art museum along Park Street and you will pass **Victoria Mansion ⊖** (109 Danforth Street; tel: 207-772-4841; www.victoriamansion. org; May–Oct Mon–Sat 10am–3.45pm, Sun 1–4.45pm), one of America's most extravagant Victorian homes.

FREEPORT

Drive 17 miles (27km) northeast out of Portland on Route 1 to **Freeport ❷**, New England's most famous outlet-mall town. The many outlet stores that line the streets arrived in the wake of **L.L. Bean** (95 Main Street; www.llbean.com; daily 24hrs), founded in 1912 by Leon Leonwood Bean as a purveyor of waterproof hunting boots. There's a café in the complex, as well as a kiosk for **Linda Bean's Perfect Maine Lobster Rolls**, see **❷**.

BRUNSWICK

Ten miles (16km) farther along Route 1 is **Brunswick ❸**, home of prestigious **Bowdoin College**, founded in 1794. Two alumni, explorers Admiral Robert E. Peary and Captain Donald MacMillan, are remembered at the **Peary-MacMillan Arctic Museum** (Hubbard Hall; tel: 207-725-3416; www.bowdoin. edu/arctic-museum; Tue–Sat 10am–5pm, Sun 2–5pm; donation). Here you will find photos, documents, and equipment from their polar expeditions.

The **Bowdoin Museum of Art** (Walker Building; tel: 207-725-3275;

Lobster fishing

www.bowdoin.edu/art-museum; Tue–Sat 10am–5pm, Thu until 8.30pm, Sun 1–5pm; donation), which has had a $20 million renovation, exhibits work by American colonial, Impressionist, and modern painters, as well as European masters.

BATH

Continue along Route 1 to the shipbuilding town of **Bath ④**, where the **Maine Maritime Museum and Shipyard** (243 Washington Street; tel: 207-443-1316; www.mainemaritimemuseum.org; daily 9.30am–5pm; charge), set in 25 acres (10ha) on the banks of the Kennebec River, chronicles the industry that keeps the town's economy ticking. Grab a bite at **Mae's Café and Bakery**, see ❸.

WISCASSET

The next stop, 9 miles (14km) farther along Route 1, is the picturesque village of **Wiscasset ⑤**, known for its Federal-style homes and antiques shops. The grand mansion **Castle Tucker** (2 Lee Street; tel: 207-882-7169; www.historicnewengland.org; June–mid-Oct Wed–Sun 11am–4pm) overlooks the Sheepscot River from atop a hill at one end of town and is worth going up to for the view. Back down by the river, enjoy a lobster roll from **Red's Eats**, see ❹.

ROCKLAND

Continue along Route 1 for 42 miles (68km) to reach **Rockland ⑥**, one of

---

Cruising the islands

The peninsulas and islands off Maine's coast are best seen from the decks of a windjammer. The schooners *Heritage* (tel: 207-594-8007; www.schoonerheritage.com) and *Victory Chimes* (tel: 1-800-745-5651; www.victorychimes.com) both sail out of Rockland. Alternatively, the Maine State Ferry (tel: 1-800-491-4883; http://maine.gov/mdot/ferry) goes to Vinalhaven and North Haven, serene islands with villages overlooking Penobscot Bay.

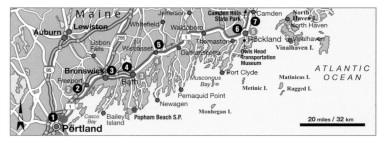

Rockland's harbor   *Looking out over Camden from Mount Battie*

Midcoast's less prettified towns, which has, nonetheless, been making a name for itself lately as a destination for art lovers and foodies. The **Maine Lobster Festival** (www.mainelobsterfestival.com) is held here at the end of July, and Rockland's working harbor is the jumping-off point for cruises and ferries to and around nearby islands (see box).

The town's **Farnsworth Art Museum** (16 Main Street; tel: 207-596-6457; www.farnsworthmuseum.org; Jan–Mar Wed–Sun 10am–4pm, Apr–May and Nov–Dec Tue–Sun 10am–5pm, June–Oct daily 10am–5pm) has an excellent American collection, and is strong on paintings by the Wyeth family. After, settle down for lunch at **Rockland Café**, see ❺.

CAMDEN

Enjoying a spectacular bayside location, **Camden** ❼, 8 miles (13km) north of Rockland, is an ideal base for touring the Midcoast. For the best panoramic view of Camden and around, head to **Camden Hills State Park** (tel: 207-236-3109; www.state.me.us; mid-May–mid-Oct dawn–dusk) and hike or drive to the summit of the 800ft (245m) **Mount Battie**.

Food and drink

❶ DUCKFAT

43 Middle Street, Portland; tel: 207-774-8080; www.duckfat.com; Sun–Thu 11am–9pm, Fri–Sat 11am–10pm; $–$$

Portlanders are rightly crazy for the Belgian-style frites with truffle ketchup that accompany panini sandwiches: try the duck confit one.

❷ LINDA BEAN'S PERFECT MAINE LOBSTER ROLLS

57 Main Street, Freeport; tel: 207-865-1874; www.lindabeansperfectmaine.com; late May–mid Oct daily 11am–6pm; $

Check out Linda's claim to the ideal roll at this takeaway kiosk.

❸ MAE'S CAFÉ AND BAKERY

160 Centre Street, Bath; tel: 207-442-8577; www.maescafeandbakery.com; daily 8am–3pm; $–$$

Drop by this convivial place for baked goods, breakfast dishes, sandwiches, and light meals.

❹ RED'S EATS

41 Water Street, Wiscasset; tel: 207-882-6128; Apr–Sept daily 11am–9pm; $

This quintessential Maine food shack has been dishing up fantastic lobster rolls and clams since the 1940s.

❺ ROCKLAND CAFÉ

441 Main Street, Rockland; tel: 207-596-7556; www.rocklandcafe.com; Nov–Apr daily 6am–8pm, May–Aug daily 5.30am–9.30pm, Sept daily 6am–9pm, Oct daily 6am–8.30pm; $–$$

Try the homemade fish cakes and other good-value seafood dishes at this friendly diner.

Acadia National Park

DOWN EAST MAINE

This beautiful, remote region is Maine at its most picturesque and rugged. Drive through attractive coastal villages to the Acadia National Park, with its granite headlands, upland meadows, pine forests, and thundering surf.

DISTANCE: 52 miles (84km) from Castine to Bar Harbor
TIME: Two to three days
START: Castine
END: Bar Harbor
POINTS TO NOTE: Bangor Airport (www.flybangor.com) is 47 miles (76km) north of Castine. Alternatively, follow on from Midcoast Maine.

CASTINE

The term 'Down East' for Maine's far northern reaches came into fashion in the 19th century, when southern New England relied on lumber shipped from here.

From Orland on Route 1, head south for 14 miles (23km) via routes 175 and 166 to begin the tour at the pretty village of **Castine ❶** (www.castine.me.us), perched on a peninsula near the head of Penobscot Bay. The ruins of **Fort George** (Battle

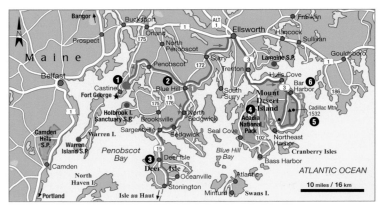

Sand Beach

Avenue) are a reminder of its historic past; the British occupied Castine during the Revolution. More than a century before that, the French had set up a trading post here. Today, tourists wander the neat grid of streets lined with Federal and Greek Revival structures, several of which are now guesthouses and restaurants.

BLUE HILL AND DEER ISLE

Twenty miles (32km) east of Castine, via routes 175 and 177, is the equally attractive town of **Blue Hill ➋** (www.town ofbluehillmaine.org), known for its galleries and crafts shops. Drop by **Cynthia Winings Gallery** (24 Parker Point Road; tel: 917-204-4001; www.cynthiawinings gallery.com; May–June Sept–Oct Tue–Sat 10.30am–5pm, July–Aug Mon–Sat 10.30am–5pm Sun noon–4pm), and the **Blue Hill Co-Op Community Market and Café**, see ➊. At this point you could drive south to Sargentville, where a causeway leads to **Deer Isle ➌**. From the fishing village of **Stonington** at the southernmost tip, you can take a ferry (tel: 207-367-5193; www.isleauhaut. com) to tranquil **Isle au Haut**. Part of this rocky island falls within Acadia National Park and is threaded with hiking trails.

ACADIA NATIONAL PARK

Accessible via causeway from Route 3, and about 24 miles (38km) from Blue Hill, much of **Mount Desert Island** is covered by the beautiful and popular **Acadia National Park ➍** (tel: 207-288-3338; www.nps.gov/acad; May–Oct). John D. Rockefeller Jr donated 10,000 acres (4,000ha) to the park and ordered the construction of the island's 58 miles (93km) of gravel-topped carriage roads, enjoyed today by hikers and mountain bikers.

Within the park, **Cadillac Mountain ➎**, at 1,532ft (467m), is the highest point on the East Coast and the first place in the nation to greet the sunrise. You can drive to the summit on a spur off the 20-mile (32km) loop road that passes other park highlights including **Sand Beach** and **Thunder Hole**. Drop by **Jordan Pond House**, see ➋, for refreshments.

Facing Frenchman Bay, bustling **Bar Harbor ➏** has attracted vacationers and the sailing crowd since the 19th century.

DIRECTORY

Hand-picked hotels and restaurants to suit all budgets and tastes, organised by area, plus select nightlife listings, an alphabetical listing of practical information, and an overview of the best books and films to give you a flavour of the region.

Balcony view from the Boston Harbor Hotel

ACCOMMODATIONS

You will seldom be far from a hotel, motel, inn, or B&B in New England, so making up a route as you go is quite feasible. However, if you want to stay at a particular place, advance reservations are recommended and are particularly important any time in summer, in the fall 'leaf-peeping' season, and near popular winter resort areas. During these times, some accommodations raise their rates and have a two-night minimum-stay policy over the weekend.

For listings of B&Bs and guesthouses in New England, check New England Inns and Resorts (www.newenglandinnsandresorts.com). Other useful websites for Boston and Massachusetts include www.boston-bnbagency.com, www.bostonhomestay.org, and www.bnbboston.com. Helpful general websites include www.visitnewengland.com, www.discovernewengland.org, and www.bnbfinder.com.

Boston (MA)

Boston Harbor Hotel
70 Rowes Wharf; tel: 617-439-7000; www.bhh.com; T-stop: Aquarium; $$$$

Price for a double room for one night without breakfast:
$$$$ = over $200
$$$ = $150–200
$$ = $75–150
$ = under $75

Board the airport water shuttle at Logan and, seven minutes later, step into one of the city's premier waterside hotels. Each of the 230 rooms has either a harbor or a skyline view. Eighteen rooms are designed for the physically disabled. Museum-quality art decorates the public areas, and the Meritage restaurant offers superb dining.

Charlesmark Hotel
655 Boylston Street; tel: 617-247–1212; http://charlesmarkhotel.com; T-stop: Copley; $$$
Location-wise, it hardly gets any better in Boston. Across the street from the Boston Public Library in Back Bay, this hotel adds to the value with stylish, albeit occasionally small, rooms spruced up by custom-made oak furniture. The outdoor patio overlooks the finish line of the Boston Marathon.

The Langham
250 Franklin Street; tel: 617-451-1900; www.langhamhotels.com; T-stop: State; $$$$
This luxurious hotel, occupying the former Federal Reserve Bank, has rooms decorated to reflect the building's opulent history. Its Café Fleuri offers a brasserie-style menu and an elaborate Sunday jazz brunch.

Liberty Hotel
215 Charles Street; tel: 617-224-4000;

The Langham's historic Federal Reserve Bank facade

http://libertyhotel.com; T-stop: Charles/
MGH; $$$$

The former Charles Street Jail (built in 1851) has been inventively renovated into this boutique hotel. Original prison catwalks and magnificent soaring windows have been preserved. The prison theme continues in the restaurant Clink and stylish bar Alibi. Also here is the contemporary Italian restaurant Scampo, run by celebrity chef Lydia Shire.

Newbury Guest House

261 Newbury Street; tel: 617-670-6000/1-
800-437-7668; www.newburyguesthouse.
com; T-stop: Hynes; $$

Three 1880s Victorian homes have been renovated to create this elegant 32-room inn. The rooms retain some of the 19th-century decorative details. There are quieter rooms in the back.

Nine Zero

90 Tremont Street; tel: 617-772-5800;
www.ninezero.com; T-stop: Park Street;
$$$$

One of Boston's sleekest boutique hotels, offering high-tech, high-speed, and high-touch amenities, along with personalized service, custom-designed beds, and down comforters. The restaurant, Highball Lounge, serves creative snacks and cocktails.

Ritz-Carlton, Boston Common

10 Avery Street; tel: 617-574-7100/1-800-
241-3333; www.ritzcarlton.com; T-stop:
Boylston; $$$$

Overlooking the Common, the modern Ritz-Carlton offers contemporary luxury minus the stuffiness that hung over its former property (now the Taj Boston) across from the Public Garden. All the rooms have modern furnishings. High tea is served in the Galleria.

Cambridge (MA)

Charles Hotel

1 Bennett Street; tel: 617-864-1200;
www.charleshotel.com; T-stop: Harvard;
$$$$

The Charles Hotel offers restrained Shaker-inspired luxury, with incredible antique quilts gracing the walls, and impeccable service. All 294 rooms are well appointed and include high-tech amenities. The Regatta Bar is a great jazz venue, and the Henrietta's Table restaurant is a mainstay of the city's gourmet circuit.

Hotel Veritas

1 Remington Street; tel: 617-520-5000;
www.thehotelveritas.com; T-stop: Harvard;
$$$$

Harvard's motto inspired the name of this hotel, but its design sense comes more from contemporary schools, with a firm boutique approach to traditional New England design and plush touches, like marble showers, Egyptian cotton linens, and heated bathroom floors.

Kendall Hotel

350 Main Street; tel: 617-577-1300;
www.kendallhotel.com; T-stop: Kendall; $$$

Boston skyline view from the Liberty Hotel

Part of the MIT neighborhood, this former fire house turned quirky boutique hotel charms with a mishmash of vintage Americana and eyebrow-raising works by regional artists. Rooms follow suit and are small but homey. The restaurant is a popular lunch spot for workers in the offices nearby.

Mary Prentiss Inn

6 Prentiss Street; tel: 617-661-2929; www.maryprentissinn.com; T-stop: Porter; $$$

This historic Greek Revival building has 20 rooms with exposed beams, shutters, and antiques; some have wood-burning fireplaces and Jacuzzis. Rates include a full breakfast and complimentary afternoon tea. There is a lush outdoor deck, and free parking.

Concord (MA)

Hawthorne Inn

462 Lexington Road; tel: 978-369-5610; www.hawthorneinnconcord.com; $$

Apart from the town's Colonial Inn (see page 49), another highly recommended overnight stay is this 1870s house opposite, which sports delightfully decorated rooms.

Salem and Cape Ann (MA)

The Addison Choate Inn

49 Broadway, Rockport; tel: 1-800-245-7543; www.addisonchoateinn.com; $$

A charming 1850s house that offers modern conveniences. It has six rooms, and there is a separate cottage with two self-catering units.

Hawthorne Hotel

18 Washington Square West, Salem; tel: 978-744-4080; www.hawthornehotel.com; $$–$$$

This Federal-style red-brick building is situated by the common and handy for all downtown attractions. The rooms are all furnished with 18th-century reproductions. Facilities include a restaurant, bar, lounge, and exercise room.

The Merchant

148 Washington Street, Salem; tel: 978-745-8100; www.themerchantsalem.com; $$$–$$$$

The 18th-century house is special for many reasons: The interior woodwork is by craftsman Samuel McIntire; George Washington once stayed here; and ghosts of tortured 'witches' supposedly haunt the halls. All the color now seems to be in the bright, whimsical décor of the boutique hotel.

Yankee Clipper Inn

127 Granite Street, Rockport; tel: 978-546-0001; www.yankeeclipperinn.com; $$$–$$$$

This 1929 Art Deco oceanfront mansion has well-appointed and charmingly decorated guest rooms (six look out to sea) and a saltwater pool.

South Shore and Cape Cod (MA)

Belfry Inn

6 Jarves Street, Sandwich; tel: 508-888-8550/1-800-844-4542; www.belfryinn.com; $$$

Three separate buildings make up this inn, but the star is the deconsecrated church (the Abbey), with six rooms named for the days of the creation. Tuesday features an incredible stained-glass 'compass' window right behind the bed.

The Brass Key

67 Bradford Street, Provincetown; tel: 508-487-9005/1-800-842-9858; www.brasskey.com; $$$

A stylish guesthouse complex made up of four converted houses surrounding a small pool. There is also a spa, and all rooms have air-conditioning.

Crow's Nest Resort

496 Shore Road, North Truro; tel: 508-487-9031; www.caperesort.com; $$–$$$

This beachfront resort stands out among the roadside motels and motor inns along the route to Provincetown for its private beach, modern facilities, and views of the bay and nearby lighthouses, often from private balconies. All units come with full kitchens.

The Dan'l Webster Inn

149 Main Street, Sandwich; tel: 508-888-3622/1-800-444-3566; www.danlwebsterinn.com; $$$$

Lodgings have been available here for guests for the last 300 years. It is named after the successful Boston lawyer and US senator. There are 48 rooms and suites, gardens, a spa, and an outdoor heated swimming pool.

Provincetown Inn

1 Commercial Street, Provincetown; tel: 508-487-9500; www.provincetowninn.com; $$

This motel-style resort is bounded by water on three sides, with its own pool and direct access to the beach. It's good value for Provincetown.

Whitfield House

26 North Street, Plymouth; tel: 508-747-6735; www.whitfieldhouse.com; $$

This charming B&B, in a house dating from 1782, offers fireplaces, antique furniture, and canopy beds in two of its three bedrooms.

The Berkshires and Pioneer Valley (MA)

Deerfield Inn

81 Main Street, Deerfield; tel: 413-774-5587; www.deerfieldinn.com; $$$

All of the rooms at this 1884 inn have period wallpaper and furnishings; some have four-poster or canopy beds. The common rooms are filled with antiques, and there's also Champney's Restaurant, featuring a contemporary American menu and 101 different Martinis.

Hotel on North

297 North St, Pittsfield; tel: 413-358-4741; http://hotelonnorth.com; $$$

A rare example of a modern boutique style in the area, this upscale hotel in a restored 1880s building in downtown Pittsfield draws its furnishings and accoutrements from the best of New England's craftsmen today.

Room at the Red Lion Inn

The Porches Inn

231 River Street, North Adams; tel: 413-664-0400; www.porches.com; $$$
This stylish inn across the road from MASS MoCA offers 47 imaginatively decorated rooms that pay quirky homage to the town's former mill workers. There's also a pool.

The Red Lion Inn

30 Main Street, Stockbridge; tel: 413-298-5545; www.redlioninn.com; $$–$$$$
It hardly gets more traditional than this historic 108-room inn, dating back to 1773 and immortalized in Norman Rockwell's painting *Stockbridge Main Street at Christmas*. Six presidents have stayed here, as well as John Wayne and Bob Dylan. Sit on the front porch and watch the world go by, or dine in its elegant restaurant hung with chandeliers.

Providence (RI)

The Dean

122 Fountain Street; tel: 401-455–3326; http://thedeanhotel.com; $$$
Formerly a strip club, this boutique hotel now caters to the hip and trendy with a minimalist, masculine vibe; sexy cocktail den; and karaoke. Rooms are on the small side, but impressively designed, with original artwork and signature black bathrooms.

Hotel Providence

311 Westminster Street; tel: 401-861-8000/1-800-861-8990; www.thehotelprovidence.com; $$$
On trendy Westminster Street is this boutique 80-room property, which has benefited from the design skills of a Rhode Island School of Design professor.

Providence Biltmore

11 Dorrance Street; tel: 401-421-0700; www.providencebiltmore.com; $$–$$$
Old World elegance at the heart of downtown Providence has been the Biltmore's stock in trade for decades. Renovations in 2015 fully restored the grande dame's glamour.

Newport (RI)

The Chanler

117 Memorial Boulevard; tel: 401-847-1300; www.thechanler.com; $$$$
Although the themed rooms are somewhat gimmicky, this cliffside hotel excels at comfort, romance, and views of Easton Bay, making it a favorite for weddings and honeymoons. The restaurant, Spiced Pear, also brings in locals for fine dining New England style.

The Hotel Viking

1 Bellevue Avenue; tel: 401-847-3300/1-800-556-7126; www.hotelviking.com; $$$–$$$$
This property on the National Register of Historic Places blends bygone detail with guest comforts. Rooms – particularly suites – are spacious and well equipped. There's a pool, hot tub, sauna, restaurant, and rooftop bar.

The Ivy Lodge

12 Clay Street; tel: 401-849-6865;

www.ivylodge.com; $$–$$$
This Victorian 'cottage' in the mansion district features a 33ft (10m) high Gothic paneled oak entrance and a three-story turned-baluster stairway. Guest rooms have private baths, period furnishings, brass or iron beds, and fireplaces. Hearty buffet-style breakfasts are included.

Connecticut Coast

Griswold Inn

36 Main Street, Essex; tel: 860-767-1776; www.griswoldinn.com; $$–$$$
Dating back to 1776, this is one of the oldest inns in the US. All rooms have private baths and period furnishings, and some have fireplaces. There is an atmospheric taproom (bar), and a restaurant that serves classic New England fare; Sunday brunch is a tradition.

Steamboat Inn

73 Steamboat Wharf, Mystic; tel: 860-536-8300; www.steamboatinnmystic.com; $$$–$$$$
This renovated riverfront warehouse is a good choice for luxurious accommodations. Big rooms have been beautifully decorated and have whirlpool baths; some of them feature wet bars and fireplaces.

Study at Yale

1157 Chapel Street, New Haven; tel: 203-503-3900; www.studyhotels.com; $$$–$$$$
A lovely, designer boutique hotel, steps away from the heart of the campus. Spacious rooms are decorated in calming colors and a tasteful mix of contemporary and traditional furnishing, including leather reading chairs.

Whalers' Inn

20 East Main Street, Mystic; tel: 860-536-1506; www.whalersinnmystic.com; $$–$$$
Located one block from the Mystic River, this complex includes a small hotel with Victorian furnishings and reproduction four-poster beds, and the fancy Italian restaurant Bravo Bravo.

The Green Mountains (VT)

The Inn at Weston

630 Main Street, Weston; tel: 802-824-6789; www.innweston.com; $$–$$$$
The original inn at this three-building complex dates from 1848. Accommodations are luxurious, with fresh-cut flowers, wood-burning fireplaces, and whirlpool tubs for two. Contemporary regional cuisine is served in the candlelit dining room.

The Latchis

50 Main Street, Brattleboro; tel: 802-275-5109; www.latchishotel.com; $$
Occupying part of a handsome 1938 Art Deco building, which also includes a beautifully preserved cinema of the era, is this great-value hotel run under the stewardship of the Brattleboro Arts Initiative – hence the work by local artists displayed in each room.

The Pitcher Inn

275 Main Street, Warren; tel: 802-496-6350; www.pitcherinn.com; $$$$

Lakeside at the Basin Harbor Club

One of the best hotels in the state, the Pitcher impresses with both its splendid location along Mad River, under the peaks of Sugarbush ski resort, and fun, whimsical ski-lodge design. Endless outdoor activities are steps from the front door.

Twin Farms
452 Royalton Turnpike, Barnard; tel: 802-234-9999; www.twinfarms.com; $$$$

Few hotel experiences in the world can match a stay at this ultra-exclusive resort set among three hundred acres of rolling hills. The 1795 farmhouse at the center was the home of Nobel Prize-winning writer Sinclair Lewis. Similar pedigree is found in the cottages, including artwork by Jasper Johns. The spa is also second to none, as are the prices.

Woodstock Inn and Resort
14 The Green, Woodstock; tel: 802-332-6853/1-888-338-2745; www.woodstockinn.com; $$$–$$$$

An elegant, historic inn has spacious guest rooms with colonial furnishings and occasional porches and/or fireplaces. Amenities include a fine restaurant, tavern, swimming pool, and nearby golf course.

Burlington and Lake Champlain Valley (VT)

Basin Harbor Club
4800 Basin Harbor Road, Vergennes; tel: 802-475-2311/1-800-622-4000; www.basinharbor.com; $$$–$$$$

This gracious lakefront resort, situated on 700 acres (283ha), has fine views across Lake Champlain and offers comfortable accommodations in cottages or in rooms and suites in lodges. Activities on offer include an 18-hole golf course, boating on the lake, children's programs, and tennis. The restaurant serves classic American cuisine; collared shirts are requested at dinner and ties and jackets preferred. Closed mid-Oct–mid-May.

The Chipman Inn
Route 125, Ripton; tel: 802-388-2390; www.chipmaninn.com; $–$$

In a tranquil spot within the Green Mountains National Forest, and close by the nature walk to poet Robert Frost's cabin, is this charming, simple inn with a private bar and spacious, country-style rooms.

Hotel Vermont
41 Cherry Street, Burlington; tel: 802-651-0080; http://hotelvt.com; $$$$

Burlington's best hotel wins effusive praise for its clever, boutique design and character that applies a 21st-century vision on classic Vermont elements, smoky black granite walls, reclaimed oak floors, and local artwork. The restaurant, Juniper, is local hangout, with some of the best cocktails in town.

Inn at Shelburne Farms
1611 Harbor Road, Shelburne; tel: 802-985-8498; www.shelburnefarms.org; $$$–$$$$

The grand 1899 Webb family mansion, on the grounds of a working farm and

The Middlebury Inn

National Historic Landmark, offers 24 luxurious, period-decorated guest rooms, an excellent library, spectacular views of Lake Champlain, and some of Vermont's finest dining. Closed mid-Oct–mid-May.

Made INN Vermont

204 South Willard Street; tel: 802-399-2788; www.madeinnvermont.com; $$$$

Few bed and breakfasts in the world pack as much quirk as this one inside a gorgeous Victorian house, starting with the record players and vinyl collection in each room, guitars and amps in the hallways, and endless shelves of artsy curiosities. The view of Lake Champlain from the widow's walk is unmatched anywhere in town.

The Middlebury Inn

14 Court Square, Middlebury; tel: 802-388-4961; www.middleburyinn.com; $$–$$$$

A rambling and creaking brick inn from 1827, with well-restored and appointed rooms in the main inn and the Victorian-era Porter House Mansion, as well as accommodations in the attached contemporary motel. Afternoon tea, included in the rates, is served daily 2.30–5.30pm.

The Lakes Region (NH)

Mill Falls at the Lake

312 Daniel Webster Highway, Meredith; 844-745-2931; http://millfalls.com; $$$$

The inviting waters of Lake Winnipesaukee are right outside the door of this resort divided into four lodgings, each with its own flavor and character, including a 40-ft waterfall running alongside. The spa is one of the best in New Hampshire.

The Wolfeboro Inn

90 North Main Street, Wolfeboro; tel: 603-569-3016; www.wolfeboroinn.com; $$$–$$$$

There are lake views from the balconies of some of the recently renovated rooms at this attractive property with a private beach beside the water. Its Wolfe's Tavern, hung with pewter mugs, is a convivial place for a relaxed meal or drink.

The White Mountains (NH)

Adair Country Inn

80 Guider Lane, Bethlehem; tel: 603-444-2600; www.adairinn.com; $$$

This luxurious Georgian Revival mansion, set in 200 acres (80ha) overlooking the Presidential Mountain range, offers 11 antiques-decorated guest rooms. The restaurant (Thu–Mon) is open to outside guests for dinner.

Adventure Suites

3440 White Mountain Highway, North Conway; tel: 603-356-9744; www.adventuresuites.com; $–$$$

Your kids (and the child inside you) will be in raptures if you check into this whacky theme hotel. All rooms are different and they include ones designed as a tree house, a log cabin, and a cave with stalactites and a waterfall shower.

AMC Highland Center

Route 302, Crawfold Notch; tel: 603-278-4453; www.outdoors.org; $

Ideal for hikers, this place offers simple shared and private accommodations and an environmental learning center. Meals are available from a self-serve canteen.

AMC Pinkham Notch Camp and Huts

Route 16, Pinkham Notch (reservations: Box 298, Gorham); tel: 603-466-2727; www.outdoors.org; $

These accommodations at the base of Mount Washington include bunk, private, and family rooms, all with shared bath. Three meals are served daily, and there's a living room with a fireplace.

Omni Mount Washington Resort

Route 302, Bretton Woods; tel: 603-278-1000/1-800-809-6664; www.omnihotels.com; $$$$

This grande dame of the White Mountains opened in 1902 and is still going strong. It offers a wide variety of accommodations, plus activities including golf, skiing, and a state-of-the-art spa. Men are requested to wear collared shirts and pressed slacks or more to dine in the formal dining room in the evening. A lovely, quieter place to stay is the resort's elegant Bretton Arms Inn.

Portsmouth (NH)

Ale House Inn

121 Bow Street; tel: 603-431-7760; www.alehouseinn.com; $$–$$$$

This recently renovated hotel occupies the second floor of an old brick brewery (hence the name). Some of the contem-porary design rooms provide glimpses of the river. No food is served, but there are plenty of places to eat nearby.

The Hotel Portsmouth

40 Court Street; tel: 603-433-1200; www.thehotelportsmouth.com; $$–$$$$

Set in a Queen Anne townhouse (and modern addition) in the city's most historic district. New ownership and renovations have endowed the property with a contemporary boutique spirit with a vintage, mid-century flavor.

Wentworth by the Sea

588 Wentworth Road, New Castle; tel: 603-422–7322/866-384–0709; www.wentworth.com; $$$$

This colossal grand dame of the Victorian age overlooks the sea and a mini archipelago of forested islands just three miles east of Portsmouth. All rooms come with ocean or harbor views, while large sunny suites with gas fireplaces occupy the newer building next to the marina. A pool and spa add more to the pampering.

Portland and Midcoast Maine

Camden Harbour Inn

83 Bayview Street, Camden; tel: 866-626-1504/1-800-236-4266; www.camdenharbourinn.com; $$$$

Enjoy lovely views, king-size feather beds, and contemporary boutique furnishings in dramatic colors at this super-stylish hotel. Also drop by for its award-winning restaurant, Natalie's (www.nataliesrestaurant.com; daily 5.30–8.30pm,

Nov–May closed Sun).

Camden Maine Stay
22 High Street, Camden; tel: 207-236-9636; www.camdenmainestay.com; $$–$$$$
This 200-year-old colonial inn has eight comfortable, air-conditioned, eclectically decorated rooms, and two parlors with wood-burning fireplaces. Full breakfast can be taken on the porch overlooking the garden.

Morrill Mansion Bed and Breakfast
249 Vaughan Street, Portland; tel: 207-774-6900/1-888-5667-7455; http://morrill mansion.com; $$–$$$
This charming 19th-century townhouse in Portland's historic West End has been beautifully restored. The seven rooms benefit from modern amenities and spa tubs.

Portland Harbor Hotel
468 Fore Street, Portland; tel: 207-775-9090/1-888-798-9090; www.portland harborhotel.com; $$$$
In the heart of the city's Old Port District, this fine hotel offers bags of character and all the amenities you could need. Some rooms open out directly onto the lovely courtyard garden.

The Press Hotel
119 Exchange Street; tel: 207-573-2425; www.thepresshotel.com; $$$–$$$$
This former newspaper building now houses a boutique hotel that pays tribute its past with rooms taking inspiration from 1920s' writer's offices, with clever typography and printing themes running throughout but all the modern bells and whistles. Maine artists and designers are well represented in the furnishings and gallery space.

Down East Maine

The Bass Cottage Inn
14 The Field, Bar Harbor; tel: 207-288-1234; www.basscottage.com; $$$$
A baby grand piano in the spacious lounge sets the tone at this gracious guesthouse, which holds back on the heritage decor that features prominently in many other Bar Harbor abodes.

The Castine Inn
33 Main Street, Castine; tel: 207-326-4365; www.castineinn.com; $–$$
Opened in 1898 and located near the harbor, the gracious Castine Inn offers spacious accommodations. Guests can enjoy the sauna, a wraparound porch, and a common room with a fireplace. The award-winning chef/owner also conducts cooking classes here.

Oceanside Meadows Inn
202 Corea Road, Prospect Harbor; 207-963-5557; www.oceaninn.com; $$$–$$$$
The décor follows the traditional New England style, with antique furniture, flowery wallpaper, and clapboard façades, but outside the door are 200 acres (81ha) of wilderness preserve teaming with moose, eagles, and more, not to mention a private sandy beach.

Top of the Hub

RESTAURANTS

Wood-paneled and beamed colonial dining rooms, retro-styled diners, sophisticated flights of culinary fancy, and seafood enjoyed within sight of the harbors where it was landed – all these experiences and more are available in the region's eclectic spread of restaurants and cafés.

Generally, there is no need to sweat about scoring a table at even the hottest chef's table. Nevertheless, you would be well advised to make an advance booking for Friday or Saturday nights; try the online booking service www.opentable.com. Note also that some places don't take reservations at all, so either turn up early or be prepared to wait.

Boston (MA)

Barcelona Wine Bar
525 Tremont Street; tel: 617-266-2600; www.barcelonawinebar.com; Mon–Fri 4pm–1am Sat–Sun 10–1am; $$–$$$
One of the international scene's best-loved restaurants in Boston, this Spanish tapas place in the trendy South End goes above and beyond, with exotic combinations like roasted beets with

---

Price for a three-course dinner for one, excluding beverages, tax, and tip:
$$$$ = over $60
$$$ = $40–60
$$ = $20–40
$ = below $20

---

pistachio pesto and roasted bone marrow in green strawberries. Pair with more than 40 wines by the glass.

Bricco Enoteca & Lounge
241 Hanover Street, North End; tel: 617-248-6800; www.bricco.com; Mon–Fri 4–11pm, Sat–Sun 4pm–2am; $$$$
This upscale boutique Italian restaurant prepares regional treats including handmade pasta. The waiters will urge you to order a 'traditional' meal with several courses, so come prepared with an empty stomach and full wallet.

Capo
443 W Broadway; tel: 617-993-8080; www.caposouthboston.com; Mon–Fri 5pm–1am, Sat–Sun 11–1am; $$
Drawing on Boston's deep cultural ties with Italy, this trendy new addition to the South End scene infuses its speakeasy-esque ambiance with a serious dose of contemporary design. The back room adds an open kitchen, wood-burning fireplace, and bar built in wood salvaged from a nearby Converse shoe factory.

The Daily Catch
323 Hanover Street, North End; tel: 617-523-8567; http://thedailycatch.com; daily 11am–10pm; $$
This tiny hole-in-the-wall institution specializes in Sicilian seafood.

Lobster at Top of the Hub

Todd English's Figs

67 Main Street, Charlestown; tel: 617-242-2229; Mon–Thu 11.30am–10pm, Fri until 10.30pm, Sat noon–10.30pm, Sun noon–9.30pm; $$

Celebrity chef Todd English's gourmet pizzeria serves excellent thin-crust pizza, grilled in wood-fired ovens and topped with a variety of epicurean toppings. The fig and prosciutto special is a favorite.

Neptune Oyster

63 Salem St; tel: 617-742-3474; www.neptuneoyster.com; Mon–Fri 11.30am–10pm, Sat–Sun until 11pm; $$$

With its long Atlantic coastline, Massachusetts has some of the best seafood available anywhere, inspiring a particular love of oysters. Just inside the North End, this demure but classy, marble-topped establishment impresses most with the variety and quality of its raw bar.

Parker's Restaurant

60 School Street; tel: 617-725-1600; (617) 725-1600; Mon–Sat 6.30am–10pm, Sun 11.30am–2pm; $$$

Dining experiences in Boston rarely get more historic, or posh, than at this nearly 170-year-old restaurant in the hotel of the same name. The Boston Cream Pie was invented here, JFK proposed to Jackie at table 40, and Malcolm X cleared dishes as a busboy. Classic fine dining menu remains.

Top of the Hub

Prudential Tower, 800 Boylston Street; tel: 617-536-1775; http://topofthehub.net; Mon–Thu 11.30am–2pm 5–10pm, Fri–Sat until 11pm, Sun 11am–2pm 5–10pm, bar daily 11.30–1am; $$$$

It's position at the tip of the Prudential Tower puts a spotlight on this fancy fine-dining affair for locals and tourists alike, making reservations sometimes essential. But there's good reason for it, with a spectacular 360-degree view of the city and coast. Soft jazz from live bands adds to the romance.

Cambridge

Algiers Coffee House

40 Brattle Street; tel: 617-492-1557; daily 8am–midnight; $$

Hang out with Harvard's boho crowd at this atmospheric, North African-styled place, serving a reasonably priced menu of well-prepared Middle Eastern standards. The falafel has a unique twist and the handmade lamb sausage is seasoned to perfection.

The Border Café

32 Church Street; 617-864-6100; www.bordercafe.com; Mon–Thu 11–1am, Fri–Sat until 2am, Sun 11am–midnight; $–$$

This 30-year stalwart remains a favorite of the Harvard area, not just because of the cheap, ample portions of Mexican classics and generously-spiked frozen margaritas, but also the fun that fills the two floors with infectious energy.

Allium

At peak dining times, this sometimes means a line out the door.

Harvest

44 Brattle Street; tel: 617-868-2255; www.harvestcambridge.com; daily 11.30am–2pm 5.30–10pm, Fri–Sat until 11pm; $$$

As the name suggests, the restaurant focuses on the region's freshest seasonal ingredients to prepare dishes interpreted from around the world. The atmosphere is relaxed, but has a distinct business account feel. It offers dining in one of the few garden terraces around Harvard Square.

Waypoint

1030 Massachusetts Avenue; tel: 617-864-2300; www.waypointharvard.com; Mon–Wed 5–11pm, Thu–Sat until 1am, Sun 10am–2.30pm 5–11pm; $$$

Tongues continue to wag about this 'coastally inspired' eatery and absinthe bar near Harvard Square. The adventurous menu adds pep to American comfort food, starting with tallow-fried peanuts and ribeye in creamed nettles and morels.

Salem and Cape Ann (MA)

Franklin Cape Ann

118 Main Street, Gloucester; tel: 978-283-7888; www.franklincafe.com; daily 5–11.30pm Fri–Sat until 1am; $$–$$$

Dine on dishes such as catfish tacos and homemade pasta at this sophisticated restaurant and bar that's the North Shore outpost of the original in Boston's trendy South End.

Red's Sandwich Shop

15 Central Street. Salem; 978-745-3527; www.redssandwichshop.com; Mon–Sat 5am–3pm, Sun 6am–1pm; $

The super generous portions served at this local breakfast and lunch joint, in business for more than 50 years, can easily fill you for the day with omelets, French toast, chicken pot pie, and Cuban sandwiches. The bright red 1698 building adds a fun, historical flavor.

South Shore and Cape Cod (MA)

The Naked Oyster

Whaler's Wharf, 410 Main Street, Hyannis; tel: 508-778–6500; www.nakedoyster.com; Mon–Sat noon–10pm; $$$

This fish and seafood restaurant and raw bar comes with its own oyster farm in nearby Barnstable, meaning daily selections as fresh as they come. Slurp them right from shell or 'dress' and bake them in herbs, cheese, and bacon. Entrées are full productions of shrimp, swordfish, and more.

Ross's Grill

Whaler's Wharf, 237 Commercial Street, Provincetown; tel: 508-487-8878; www.rossgrillptown.com; Thu–Sun noon–9pm; $$$

Intimate and friendly Ross's is the epitome of relaxed fine dining, with excellent bistro-style dishes such as steak

Seafood is a staple of New England cooking

frites and crispy Tuscan cod. Offers a wide selection of wines by the glass.

Sal's Place
99 Commercial Street, Provincetown; tel: 508-487-1279; www.salsplaceprovince town.com; mid-June–mid-Sept daily 5.30–10pm; $$
When other places are booked up, it is often possible to squeeze in at Sal's, an authentic Italian joint in the West End with a romantic beachside terrace. The portions are huge and always come with a side order of pasta.

The Berkshires and Pioneer Valley (MA)

'6 House Pub
910 Cold Spring Road, Williamstown; tel: 413-458-1896; www.6housepub.com; Mon–Fri 5–10pm, Sat–Sun 11am–10pm; $$
At first glance this seems like yet another handsome, wood-paneled country pub, but further inspection reveals oodles of quirk, particularly in the upholstery. The menu follows suit, too, with dishes like 'Lobster Martini' served alongside classic burgers and sandwiches.

Allium
42–44 Railroad Street, Great Barrington; tel: 413-528-2118; www.alliumberkshires.com; Sun–Thu 5–9.30pm, Fri–Sat until 10pm; $$–$$$
The best of local ingredients are used for the appealing modern American dishes served at this relaxed restaurant, a star-pick among local foodies.

Bizen
17 Railroad Street, Great Barrington; tel: 413-528-4343; daily noon–2.30pm, 5–9.30pm Sat–Sun until 3pm and 10pm; $$$–$$$$
A fine Japanese restaurant in the Berkshires? You'd better believe it – customers and critics rave about the quality of the sushi and other traditional dishes with quirky Americanized names.

Truc Orient Express
3 Harris Street, West Stockbridge; tel: 413-232-4204; daily 11am–10pm; $$
Creative dishes, such as 'Happy Pancake' and 'Shaking Beef,' are elegantly presented in this upscale Vietnamese restaurant.

Providence (RI)

Bravo
123 Empire Street; tel: 401-490-5112; www.bravo-providence.com; Mon–Tue 5–10pm, Wed–Thu 5–11pm, Fri 11.30am–11pm, Sat 11am–11.30pm, Sun 11am–10pm; $$$
Freshly baked baguettes set the tone at this American bistro inspired by French-style cafés.

Gracie's
194 Washington Street; tel: 401-272–7811; http://graciesprov.com; Tue–Sat 5–10pm; $$$
There's a little romance in the air, along with the aroma of upscale American fish, seafood, and meat dishes, at this woody, white table-clothed restaurant.

Many of the dishes' ingredients come from a rooftop garden.

Nick's on Broadway

500 Broadway; tel: 401-421-0286; http://nicksonbroadway.com; Wed–Sat 8am–3pm 5.30–10pm bar until 11pm, Thu–Fri bar until midnight, Sun 8am–3pm; $$$

Just 24 years old when he opened Nick's in 2002, chef Derek Wagner has built this restaurant into one of Providence's best, with seasonally inspired, locally-sourced new American cuisine. Think tallow-roasted potatoes, beetroot hummus, and chargrilled Berkshire pork.

Waterman Grille

4 Richmond Square; tel: 401-521-9229; www.watermangrille.com; Mon–Thu 4–9pm, Fri until 10pm, Sat 10am–3pm 4pm–10pm, Sun 10am–9pm; $$$

Any discussion of this elegant seaside restaurant must begin with the views of the Seekonk River, flowing almost underneath. It gets even better on the outdoor terrace, especially with a glass of wine and a wood-grilled filet mignon.

Newport (RI)

Castle Hill Inn

590 Ocean Drive, tel: 401-849-3800; www.castlehillinn.com; Sun–Thu 5.45–9pm, Fri–Sat until 10pm; $$$$

One of the best views in Newport is from a table of this upscale inn atop a forty-acre peninsula facing the Atlantic. The best are in the Sunset Room, one of four dining rooms inside the 19th-century inn, and menu matches with international dishes infused with local ingredients and tastes.

Salvation Café

140 Broadway; tel: 401-847-2620; www.salvationcafe.com; daily 5–11pm; $$

With a fun menu and decor that hops around the world for inspiration, and reasonable prices for upmarket Newport, this is a cool place to hang out. The bar serves drinks until midnight.

The Spiced Pear

The Chanler at Cliff Walk, 117 Memorial Boulevard; tel: 401-847-2244.; www.thechanler.com; late May–TK daily 12.30–3.30pm 5.30–8.30pm; $$$$

If you are going to push the boat out, do it in style with the delicious gourmand tasting menu at this super-elegant restaurant, part of a luxurious boutique hotel. In good weather dine on the verandah with ocean views.

White Horse Tavern

26 Marlborough Street; tel: 401-849-3600; www.whitehorsetavern.us; Sun–Thu 11am–9pm, Fri–Sun until 10pm; $$$

The country's oldest operating tavern (1673) serves fine-dining American cuisine, with dishes such as Vermont goat's cheesecake, New England lobster sauté, and Georges Bank flounder.

Connecticut coast

Café Routier

1353 Boston Post Road, Old Saybrook; tel:

860-399-8700; www.caferoutier.com; Sun–
Thu 5–9pm, Fri–Sat until 10pm; $$$
Artfully prepared French and American
dishes, a fine wine list, and candlelit
tables with white linen tablecloths all
contribute to this restaurant's classy
reputation.

Claire's Corner Copia

1000 Chapel Street, New Haven; tel: 203-
562–3888; www.clairescornercopia.com;
Mon–Fri 8am–9pm, Sat–Sun 9am–9pm; $
Since 1975, this New Haven institution
has been feeding the region's vegetar-
ians and vegans, with frittatas, sand-
wiches, salads, and quesadillas. The
Lithuanian coffee cake is a local favorite.

Modern Apizza

874 State St, New Haven; tel: 203-776-
5306; http://modernapizza.com; Tue–Thu
11am–10pm, Fri–Sat 11am–11pm, Sun
3–10pm; $
Some might consider it a criminal
offence to leave New Haven without at
least one steaming pie from this legend-
ary pizza joint, opened in 1934. All the
classics are represented, plus a host of
'specialty' pizzas made with a mozza-
rella base.

Burlington and Lake Champlain Valley (VT)

A Single Pebble

133 Bank Street, Burlington; tel: 802-
865-5200; http://asinglepebble.com;
Sun–Fri 11.30am–1.45pm 5pm–9pm, Sat
11am–3pm 5pm–10pm; $$$

Burlington's top spot for Asian com-
bines the flavors of the Silk Road into
high-end classical Chinese dishes, with
its mock eel (made of shitake mush-
rooms) earning a shout out on the Food
Network's *The Best Thing I Ever Ate*.

American Flatbread

115 Saint Paul Street, Burlington; tel: 802-
861-2999; http://americanflatbread.com;
Mon–Fri 11.30am–3pm 5pm–11.30pm,
Sat–Sun 11.30am–11.30pm; $$
Arguably the best pizzas in the state
come from the wood-fired, domed, clay-
and-stone ovens here. As the baking
takes place directly adjacent the dining
area, the ovens, and their team of pad-
dlers, also provide the entertainment.
The restaurant also has branches in
Middlebury and Waitsfield.

Bearded Frog

5247 Shelburne Road, Shelburne; tel:
802-985-9877; www.thebeardedfrog.com;
Sun–Wed 5–8.30pm, Thu until 9pm, Fri–Sat
until 10pm; $$$
Located in a restored 19th-century farm-
house, this gastropub serves dishes as
diverse as crunchy tofu cakes and but-
termilk-marinated pork chops.

Guild Tavern

1633 Williston Rd, South Burlington; tel:
802-497-1207; www.guildtavern.com;
Sun–Thu 4.30pm–9pm, Fri–Sat until 10pm;
$$–$$$$
The Guild grills up possibly the best
steaks in Vermont, carved from grass-

The Simon Pearce Restaurant

fed, grain-finished steers at LaPlatte River Angus Farm in neighboring Shelburne. More than 20 Vermont farms supply the rabbit, pork, chicken, veggies, and cheese for the rest of the menu.

Juniper
115 Church Street, Burlington; tel: 41 Cherry Street; http://hotelvt.com; Mon–Thu 7am–2pm 5pm–10pm, Fri–Sat until midnight; $$$
The house restaurant of the swanky Hotel Vermont has become a destination of its own, thanks to its woody, boutique ambiance, creative new American cuisine, and some of the best cocktails in the state. The outdoor patio has views of the lake, and a fire pit.

Leunig's Bistro
115 Church Street, Burlington; tel: 802-863-3759; www.leunigsbistro.com; Mon–Thu 11am–10pm, Fri–Sat 11am–11pm, Sun 9am–10pm; $$
Art Deco rules at this atmospheric French bistro with a fine menu.

The Green Mountains (VT)

Chelsea Royal Diner
487 Marlboro Road, West Brattleboro; tel: 802-254-8399; www.chelsearoyaldiner. com; daily 5.30am–9pm; $
Against the backdrop of forests and mountains, this handsome, wood-covered, 1938 Worcester Diner still dishes out the classic blue plate specials but with serious attention to fresh, local, and humane sourcing.

Hen of the Wood
92 Stowe Street, Waterbury; tel: 802-244-7300; http://henofthe wood.com; Tue–Sat 5pm–9pm; $$$
Considered by many the best restaurant in Vermont, Hen of the Wood wows its fans both with a romantic setting in an 1835 grist mill and ultra-fresh regional menu, assiduously determined by what's available daily from its network of local sources.

Mary's Restaurant
1868 North 116 Road, Bristol; tel 802-453-2432; www.baldwincreek. net; May–Oct Wed–Sat 5–8.30pm, Sun 10.30am–2pm 5–8.30pm, Nov–Apr Wed–Sat 5–8.30pm, Sun 10.30am–2pm
Located just outside Bristol, at the south end of scenic Route 116, this hotel restaurant stands well on its own, with forests and mountains surrounding to boot. Adopting a 'slow food' philosophy, they serve creative takes on local, naturally raised beef, pork, lamb, rabbit, venison and chicken.

Simon Pearce Restaurant
1760 Quechee Main Street, Quechee; tel: 802-295-1470; www.simonpearce.com; daily 11.30am–2.45pm 5.30–9pm, Sun from 10.30am; $$$$
A short drive out of Woodstock is this lovely restaurant in an old mill overlooking the Ottauquechee River. Fine country cuisine is prepared using local produce.

Cod dish at the Simon Pearce Restaurant

T.J. Buckley's

132 Elliot Street, Brattleboro; tel: 802-257-4922; http://tjbuckleysuptowndining.com; Thu–Sun 5.30–9.30pm; $$$

Typical of this quirky town is this eight-table restaurant serving top-flight cuisine out of a snug little 1927 diner.

The Lakes Region (NH)

Corner House Inn

22 Main Street, Center Sandwich; tel: 603-284-6219; www.cornerhouseinn.com; Mon Wed–Thu 4.30–9pm, Fri–Sat until 10pm, Sun 11.30–9pm; $$

This converted harness from 1849 shop embraces north country quirk with paintings by local artists and storytelling dinners every Thursday. The menu covers classic sirloins, scampis, and burgers, with ingredients sourced from local farm stands.

The Crystal Quail

202 Pitman Road, Center Barnstead; tel: 603-269–4151; www.crystalquail.com; Wed–Sun 5–9pm; $$$$

People speak of the Crystal Quail as almost a legend, but this rural 18th-century farmhouse restaurant of just four tables is real indeed, and one of New Hampshire's most memorable dining experiences. The prix-fixe menu of regional dishes changes daily but sources from as close as the garden outside.

Shibley's At the Pier

42 Mt. Major Highway, Alton Bay; tel: 603-875-3636; mid-April–mid-Oct daily 5–9pm,

mid-Jan–mid Apr Fri–Sat 11am–9pm Sun 11am–4pm; $$$

Pause at this humble pit stop for 24 flavors of soft-serve ice cream, plus burgers or sandwiches, which you can take across the road to enjoy beside the lake.

The White Mountains (NH)

The 1785 Inn

3582 White Mountain Highway, Intervale; tel: 603-356-9025; www.the1785inn.com; daily 5–9pm; $$$

With a huge fireplace and a colonial atmosphere, this inn has an extensive list of appetizers, creative continental entrées, and a superb wine list.

Gypsy Café

117 Main Street, Lincoln; tel: 603-745-4395; www.gypsycaferestaurant.com; daily 11.30am–4pm 5–9pm; $$

The visual delights of this eclectic café, stuffed with local art, enhance the impressive work on the menu, which remixes New England and international cuisine. Think cranberry mac-and-cheese and Ethiopian Peppercorn Sirloin.

Le Rendez Vous

121 Main Street, Colebrook; tel: 603-237–5150; www.lerendezvousbakerynh.com; Tue–Sat 9am–5.30pm; $

It's usually a surprise for anyone to find such excellent French pastries so far north, but a pleasant one indeed. It's thanks to the café's Parisian owners,

Eating at Portland Harbour

who prepare the 12 kinds of Madeleines, macaroons, croissants, freshly breads, and fudge.

Sugar Hill Inn

116 New Hampshire 117, Sugar Hill; tel: 603-823–5621; http://sugarhillinn.com; $$$$

It's not just the no-kids policy that keeps this place romantic, but also the 1789 farmhouse setting, white clothed-tables, and fresh regional dishes sourced from the hotel's own gardens.

Portsmouth (NH)

Black Trumpet

29 Ceres Street; tel: 603-431-0887; www.blacktrumpetbistro.com; Sun–Thu 5–9pm, Fri–Sat until 10pm; $$$

Some of Portsmouth's most creative cooking takes place in the kitchens here. The family-owned bistro and wine bar romances with a cozy red-brick and dark wood interior and New American dishes, like lamb shoulder with Tunisian couscous and house-made fettucine in carrot-feta cream sauce.

Figtree Kitchen Café

14 Hancock Street; tel: 603-766-4300; www.figtreekitchen.com; daily 10am–5pm; $

If baking ranks high on the list of your culinary fetishes, this café in the Strawbery Banke Museum can satisfy with small-batch scones, cookies, baby cakes, and tarts or larger hot sandwiches, salads, and quesadillas. Sources are often local and therefore fresh.

Jumpin' Jay's Fish Café

150 Congress Street; tel: 603-766-3474; www.jumpinjays.com; Sun–Thu 5–9pm, Fri–Sat 5–10pm; $$$

The catch of the day factor's prominently in the fish and seafood heavy menu of this downtown restaurant, two blocks from Market Square. That also means a top-notch raw bar.

The Library Restaurant

401 State Street; tel: 603-431-5202; http://libraryrestaurant.com; daily 11.30am–3pm, 5–9.30pm, Fri–Sat until 10pm; $$–$$$

A wood-paneled steakhouse in elegant Rockingham House, built in 1785.

Portland and Midcoast Maine

Back Bay Grill

65 Portland Street; tel: 207-772-8833; http://backbaygrill.com; Tue–Sat 5–10pm; $$$

The James Beard Foundation counts itself one of the many fans of this upscale American bistro, kept under the radar by its location off the tourist paths. This being Maine, fish and seafood factor in several entrées. The wine list is particularly notable and one of the best in the state.

Eventide

288 Fore Street, Portland; tel: 207-774-

8538; www.eventideoysterco.com; daily 11am–midnight; $$

Raw bar fans will be hard-pressed to find a better one than this. Oysters on a half shell come in more than a dozen varieties, with the rest of the sea represented in stews, battered filets, sandwiches, and ceviche.

Five Fifty-Five

555 Congress Street, Portland; tel: 207-761-0555; www.fivefifty-five.com; daily 5–9.30pm, Fri–Sat until 10.30pm, Sun 9.30am–2pm; $$$–$$$$

The truffled lobster 'mac and cheese' is decadent, and don't miss out on delicious modern remakes of old classics, such as roasted Long Island duck and braised short rib.

Fore Street

288 Fore Street, Portland; tel: 207-775-2717; www.forestreet.biz; daily 5.30–10pm, Fri–Sat until 10.30pm; $$$–$$$$

One of the many successful restaurants that have refocused attention on Portland's Old Port District. A changing daily menu reflects all the great produce that's available in this city, with an emphasis on grilled meats and fish.

Primo

25 Main Street, Rockland; tel: 207-596-0770; www.primorestaurant.com; early May–Oct Wed–Sun 5.30–9pm, July–Aug also Mon; $$$$

Featuring seasonal produce from its own gardens, this top-class restaurant is based inside a Victorian home and has transformed Rockland into a foodie destination.

Down East Maine

Café This Way

14.5 Mount Desert Street, Bar Harbor; tel: 207-288-4483; http://cafethisway.com; May–Oct Mon–Sat 7–11.30am, Sun 8am–1pm, daily 5.30–9pm; $$–$$$

If you don't make it to this local favorite for breakfast, you get a second chance at dinner to sample the fun atmosphere and menu, featuring dishes such as smoked duck-wrapped scallops.

Pentagöet Inn

26 Main Street, Castine; tel: 207-326-8616; www.pentagoet.com; late May-late October daily 5.30–9.30pm; $$$–$$$$

This Victorian inn not only has charming rooms, but also a top-class kitchen turning out delicious meals using local produce. The cozy The Baron Pub and Wine Bar is hung with vintage photos and paintings.

Chowder House

167 Water Street, Eastport; tel: 207-853-4700; www.eastportchowderhouse.org; daily TKTKTK; $

The views of the Bay of Fundy and Atlantic islands form the picturesque backdrop of the seaside restaurant built in an old cannery. That means lots of fresh fish and seafood whipped into dishes like crab cakes, grilled scallops, and fried clams.

Paradise Rock Club

NIGHTLIFE

Pubs and lounges typically open daily around 4 or 5pm. In Boston, by law, they all have to stop serving alcohol at 2am (1am Sun–Wed in Cambridge). Elsewhere in New England bar opening hours may be longer.

Connecticut is home to a couple of giant Vegas-style casinos on Native American reservations land. They offer a range of big-name entertainment to draw customers in for the gambling. Foxwoods (tel: 1-800-369-9663; www.foxwoods.com) is the world's largest casino, and there's also Mohegan Sun (tel: 888-226-7711; www.mohegansun.com

Boston (MA)

Berklee College of Music
1140 Boylston Street; tel: 617-266-1400; www.berklee.edu
Founded in 1945, this is the world's largest independent music college with a highly regarded jazz program attracting students from around the globe. Faculty, student, and recording artists regularly perform in the college's many venues.

Boston Symphony Hall
301 Massachusetts Avenue; tel: 617-266-1200; www.bso.org
The acoustically impeccable 1900 building is home to the renowned Boston Symphony Orchestra and, in summer (when the BSO performs at Tanglewood in Lenox) and during the Christmas holidays, its less formal offshoot, the Boston Pops Orchestra. Tickets can be hard to come by.

Boch Center
270 Tremont Street; tel: 617-482-9393; www.bochcenter.org
Comprising both the historic Wang and Shubert theaters, this is a focus for the major performing arts in Boston.

Bukowski Tavern
50 Dalton Street; tel: 617-437-9999; http://bukowskitavern.net
Long a favorite watering hole of the young and hip, this pub carved into the side of a parking garage is renowned for its extensive beer list and cheap, delicious eats.

Club Café
209 Columbus Avenue; tel: 617-536-0966; www.clubcafe.com
A popular gay complex and the place to be on Thursday nights, with a quieter bar and restaurant at the front and thumping music videos in the back.

Good Life
28 Kingston Street; tel: 617-451-2622; www.goodlifebar.com
A popular after-work bar with an impressive vodka menu and inventive nibbles. Walls act as a regularly changing gallery of art and DJs energize the often packed dance floor.

Club Passim

Jacob Wirth

31 Stuart Street; tel: 617-338-8586;
http://jacobwirth.com
This time-warp pub and restaurant in the Theater District, established in 1868, serves an impressive list of beers.

Jordan Hall, New England Conservatory

30 Gainsborough Street; tel: 617-585-1260;
http://necmusic.edu
This music school hosts the Boston Philharmonic as well as guest orchestras and chamber music concerts.

Paradise Rock Club

967–969 Commonwealth Avenue; tel 617-562-8800; http://crossroadspresents.com
Boston's top venue for established and up-and-coming rock and alternative pop music.

Wilbur Theatre

246 Tremont Street; tel: 617-248-9700;
http://thewilbur.com
This 1914 theater is currently home to the long-running Comedy Connection, showcasing top comedians and singers.

Cambridge (MA)

Charlie's Kitchen

10 Eliot Street; tel: 617-492-9646;
www.charlieskitchen.com
Although hipper craft brew pubs fill the Harvard neighborhood, this old school diner, in business since 1951, still packs in fans for its cheap eats, backyard beer garden, and 'best jukebox in Cambridge.'

Club Passim

47 Palmer Street; tel: 617-492-7679;
www.passim.org;
The US's oldest folk club hosts a variety of local and national artists, focusing on folk, world, and bluegrass music.

Loeb Drama Center

64 Brattle Street; tel: 617-547-8300;
http://americanrepertorytheater.org
Home of the American Repertory Theater, which presents classic and first-run drama.

Regatta Bar

Charles Hotel, 1 Bennett Street; tel: 617-661-5000; www.regattabarjazz.com
A fashionable bar on the third floor of the Charles Hotel, featuring top jazz and R&B acts in a sophisticated interior. Bookings recommended.

South Shore and Cape Cod (MA)

Atlantic House

6 Masonic Place, Provincetown; tel: 508-487-3821; www.ahouse.com
The playwright Eugene O'Neil once drank here. It's now a popular gay complex of a couple of bars and dance club with a variety of theme nights.

Cape Cod Melody Tent

21 West Main Street, Hyannis; tel: 508-775-5630; www.melodytent.org
This tent theater presents a mixture of top musical and comedy acts from across the spectrum.

Ballet at the Jacob's Pillow Dance Festival

The Berkshires and Pioneer Valley (MA)

City Stage & Symphony Hall
1 Columbus Center, Springfield; tel: 413-788-7033; www.symphonyhall.com
The 2,611-seat Symphony Hall hosts Broadway-style theater and classical concerts, while the Blake Theatre stages musicals, drama, and comedy.

Jacob's Pillow Dance
358 George Carter Road (Route 20), Becket; tel: 413-243-0745; www.jacobspillow.org
An international dance center, which presents ballet and modern works and holds a renowned summer festival.

Shakespeare and Company
70 Kemble Street, Lenox; tel: 413-637-3353; www.shakespeare.org
This venue's summer drama season showcases the Bard's works as well as contemporary playwrights.

Providence (RI)

The Magdalenae Room
122 Fountain Street; tel: 401-455-3326; http://thedeanhotel.com
Inside the boutique Dean Hotel is perhaps Providence's best cocktail bar. The speakeasy ambiance oozes sex appeal, making it perfect for a date.

Mirabar
15 Elbow Street; tel: 401-331-6761
A gay bar with a variety of theme nights, including retro and karaoke.

Red Fez
49 Peck Street; tel: 401-861-3825
Dark lighting, red walls, animal heads, and an interesting student crowd are features of this hip little restaurant/bar.

Newport (RI)

Newport Blues Café
286 Thames Street; tel: 401-841-5510; www.newportblues.com
Newport's best blues venue.

Connecticut coast

Bar
254 Crown Street, New Haven; tel: 203-495-1111; www.barnightclub.com
An attractive brew pub and club, where you can wash down pizza with the beers, play pool, or dance to the DJ's mix.

Goodspeed Opera House
6 Main Street, East Haddam; tel: 860-873-8668; www.goodspeed.org
This magnificent opera house presents plays and musicals (Apr–Dec).

Yale Repertory Theatre
Chapel and York streets, New Haven; tel: 203-432-1234; www.yalerep.org
The Yale Rep puts on quality classic and première performances.

The Green Mountains (VT)

Weston Playhouse
Village Green, Weston; tel: 802-824-5288; www.westonplayhouse.org
The Weston puts on Broadway material from June to early September.

Romeo and Juliet performed by Shakespeare and Company

Burlington (VT)

Flynn Theatre for the Performing Arts
153 Main Street; tel: 802-652-4500;
www.flynncenter.org
A restored Art Deco building hosting the Vermont Symphony, drama, and big-name performers.

Nectar's
188 Main Street; tel: 802-658-4771;
http://liveatnectars.com
This long-running music bar and restaurant showcases hot local groups, several of whom, particularly Phish, have gone on to international fame.

Vermont Comedy Club
101 Main Street; tel: 802-859-0100;
http://vermontcomedyclub.com
This 150-seat space inside an old armory welcomes national and local comics to the mic, as well as conducting classes and workshops in the art of comedy.

Portsmouth (NH)

Earth Eagle Brewings
165 High Street; tel: 603 502-2244;
http://eartheaglebrewings.com
Portsmouth's leading craft brew pub pours an ever rotating collection of pilsners, pale ales, stouts, porters, and gruits. Take it outside to the beer garden.

The Press Room
77 Daniel Street; tel: 603-431-5186;
www.pressroomnh.com
Live blues, jazz, folk, R&B, and Latin jazz are performed here seven nights a week.

Portland and Midcoast Maine

Blue
650 Congress Street, Portland; tel: 207-774-4111; http://portcityblue.com
This intimate live venue in the heart of Portland's Arts District hosts Jazz, Celtic, Middle Eastern, Blues, Bluegrass, Old Time, and Folk concerts.

Gritty's
396 Fore Street, Portland; tel: 207-772-2739; www.grittys.com
Portland's original brew pub serves its own fine ales with both typical British pub fare and local seafood dishes.

Vena's Fizz House
345 Fore Street, Portland; tel: 207-747-4901; http://venasfizzhouse.com
This cocktail bar exudes turn-of-the-20th-century charm with its brick and oak, while drinks such as the Lumber-sexual mix in 21st-century artinsanality and fun.

Waterworks
7 Lindsey Street, off Main Street, Rockland; tel: 207-596-2753
A good spot for a Maine microbrew and a bar meal or snack.

Down East Maine

The Grand
165 Main Street, Ellsworth; 207-667-9500;
http://grandonline.org
More than 200 events, including musicals, concerts, and films, take place each year at this historic Art Deco theater.

Massachusetts State House

A–Z

A

Age restrictions

The age of consent is 16 throughout New England, and you have to be 21 to drink legally in each of the six states. To drive, you need to be 16 in Connecticut, Vermont, and Maine, 17 in New Hampshire, and 18 in Massachusetts and Rhode Island.

B

Budgeting

It will cost around $7 for a beer or a glass of house wine. A main course at a budget restaurant runs to around $10, at a moderate one $25, and at an expensive one over $25.

Budget, moderate, and deluxe accommodations are under $75, between $75–200, and over $200, respectively.

Be aware that in Boston, prices usually come in at 20 percent higher than elsewhere for the same accommodations.

A taxi from Boston's Logan Airport to a hotel in the Back Bay area will cost around $33. Single bus and subway tickets in Boston cost $2 and $2.25, but are reduced to $1.70 and $1.70 if you buy a Charlie Card (see page 132).

C

Children

It is easy to travel in New England with kids. There are hands-on museums, state and theme parks, and toy- and bookstores throughout the region; and, with good planning, driving distances between destinations can be kept relatively short. Note that laws in each state are quite specific about driving with children in a car. Be sure to tell the car-rental agency in advance how old your children are, so that they will have the proper-size car seats available, and check with them about state requirements.

Many restaurants offer kids' menus, but some – particularly more expensive ones – may not welcome young children at dinner. Lodgings generally welcome children, and do not charge for those under 18, although $10 or $15 may be added to the bill for a cot or crib.

Clothing

In winter, warm clothes and waterproof shoes are a must. For all other seasons, assume that you will encounter at least one cool spell, and carry a sweater or light jacket. Raingear is advisable, particularly in spring. For climate information, see page 10.

Red Sox fans

Like the rest of the US, New England has grown increasingly less formal over recent years, and casual clothing will see you through most situations. However, shorts, jeans, and T-shirts are still frowned upon in many of the better restaurants, particularly in cities; the finest Boston establishments – as well as a few traditional mountain, seaside, and lake resorts – still expect jackets (and, in a few cases, ties) for men. A neat pair of khakis together with a blazer is virtually fail-safe; women should not encounter any problems with a casual dress or pantsuit.

Crime and safety

Boston is one of the safest cities in the US, but visitors should always be vigilant. Areas where crime is a problem offer few tourist attractions and are on the fringes of the city. Equally, New England's urban areas are among the safest in the US. Nevertheless, always lock car doors, and don't leave valuables visible in your car or hotel room.

Customs

Anyone over 21 may bring 200 cigarettes, 100 cigars, or 3lbs of tobacco, 1 liter of alcohol, and a maximum of $100 worth of duty-free gifts. Importing meat products, seeds, plants, or fruits is illegal, as are narcotics. You may take out anything you wish, but consult with the authorities of your destination country for its customs regulations on entry.

D

Disabled travelers

Boston caters well to the disabled traveler, with accessible bathrooms and ramps on public buildings, curbsides, and at most attractions. However, it is also an old city with colonial buildings and cobblestone sidewalks, so despite best efforts it is not always perfect. Check the Massachusetts Bay Transit Authority's website (www.mbta.com) for public transport access information for disabled travelers, including details of its The Ride service for door-to-door paratransit. For more information, call tel: 617-222-5123 or TTY 617-222-5415. Boston's Commission for Persons with Disabilities can be reached on tel: 617-635-3682 or via www.boston.gov/departments/disabilities-commission.

Elsewhere in New England the situation is similar. Consult Mobility International USA (www.miusa.org), and the Society for Accessible Travel & Hospitality (http://sath.org).

E

Electricity

The US uses 110–120V, 60-cycle AC voltage (as opposed to the 220–240V, 50-cycle of Europe). Laptops and many travel appliances are dual-voltage and will work, but check first. An adapter will be needed for US sockets.

Penobscot Bay lighthouse

Embassies and consulates

Most embassies are based in Washington, DC, but many countries have consulates in Boston; a complete list can be found at www.embassypages.com/city/boston.

Embassies
Australia: 1601 Massachusetts Avenue, Washington, DC; tel: 202-797-3000; www.usa.embassy.gov.au.

Consulates
Canada: 3 Copley Place, Suite 400; tel: 617-247-5100; www.can-am.gc.ca.
Ireland: 535 Boylston Street; tel: 617-267-9330; www.dfa.ie.
UK: 1 Broadway, Cambridge; tel: 617-245-4500; www.gov.uk

Emergency number

Ambulance, Fire, and Police: tel: 911.

Green issues

While many urban centers in New England practice recycling, the six states have a patchy record when it comes to environmental protection; the needs of industry and commerce have often trumped green considerations. The Conservation Law Foundation works to solve the most pressing environmental problems facing New England; its achievements have included protecting the Georges Bank from oil drilling and overfishing, ending decades of sewage dumping into Boston Harbor, preserving Vermont's bear habitats, and saving New Hampshire's Franconia Notch from a four-lane highway.

Air travel produces a huge amount of carbon dioxide and is a significant contributor to global warming. If you would like to offset the damage caused to the environment by your flight, a number of organizations can do this for you using online 'carbon calculators' that tell you how much you need to donate. In the UK travelers can visit www.climatecare.org or www.carbonneutral.com; in the US log on to www.climatefriendly.com or http://sustainabletravel.org.

Health and medical care

Sunburn will be the most common medical nuisance for most visitors. Even so, don't leave home without travel insurance to cover yourself and your belongings. It is not cheap to get sick in the United States.

Tap water is safe to drink, but avoid stream water as it can cause giardia, an intestinal disorder spread by wild animal wastes. Use a filter or purification tablets, or boil water, when hiking or camping.

Pharmacies. These stock most standard medication (although some painkillers that are available over the counter in other countries may be prescription-only in the US), and staff are trained to help

Getting ready to sunbathe on a Rhode Island beach

with most minor ailments. Across New England you will find branches of the pharmacy CVS (www.cvs.com). A central one in Boston is: 587 Boylston Street; tel: 617-437-8414.

Hospitals. These are signposted on highways with a white H on a blue background. Major hospitals have 24-hour emergency rooms; you may have a long wait before you get to see the doctor, but the care and treatment are thorough and professional.

Walk-in clinics are commonplace in cities, where you can consult a nurse or doctor for a minor ailment without an appointment. If cost is a concern, turn first to clinics offering free or pro-rated care (look then up in the Yellow Pages).

Major hospitals include:

Connecticut: Hartford Hospital, 80 Seymour Street; tel: 860-545 5000; https://hartfordhospital.org.

Maine: Maine Medical Center, 22 Bramhall Street, Portland; tel: 207-662-0111; www.mmc.org.

Massachusetts: Massachusetts General Hospital, 55 Fruit Street, Boston; tel: 617-726-2000; www.mass general.org.

New Hampshire: Portsmouth Regional Hospital, 333 Borthwick Avenue; tel: 603-436-5110.

Rhode Island: Rhode Island Hospital, 593 Eddy Street, Providence; tel: 401-444-4000; www.rhodeislandhospital. org.

Vermont: University of Vermont Medical Center, 111 Colchester Avenue, Burl-ington; tel: 802-847-0000; www.uvm health.org.

Hours and holidays

Most offices open Mon–Fri 9am–5pm. Federal and local government offices usually open Mon–Fri 8.30am–4.30pm. Banks open Mon–Fri 9am–4pm. Some also open until 5pm on Thu and Sat 9am–noon.

Public holidays

All government offices, banks, and post offices are closed on public holidays. Public transportation does not run as often on these days, but most shops, museums, and attractions are open.

Jan 1 – New Year's Day
Third Mon Jan – Martin Luther King Jr. Day
Third Mon Feb – President's Day
Mar/Apr – Easter Sunday
Third Mon Apr – Patriots' Day
Last Mon May – Memorial Day
July 4 – Independence Day
First Mon Sept – Labor Day
Second Mon Oct – Columbus Day
Last Thu and Fri Nov – Thanksgiving
Dec 25 – Christmas

Internet

Throughout New England wireless internet access is nearly ubiquitous in cafés, restaurants, pubs, many student-type hangouts, and plenty of hotels and guesthouses, and most

public libraries allow free access via their computer terminals.

L

LGBTQ travel

Massachusetts is famous as the first US state to legalize same-sex marriage. In general, Boston is a very integrated city, so you will find people of all orientations mingling in many city neighborhoods. The South End has the highest concentration of gay bars and is also the home of the annual Boston Pride parade. The National Gay and Lesbian Chamber of Commerce (http://nglcc. org) has information on businesses owned, operated, or supported by the local gay community in New England.

Northampton in Massachusetts emerged as a lively enclave for gay women in the late 20th century, and Provincetown on Cape Cod has long been one of the country's best-known gay summer vacation spots. You will also find sizeable LGBTQ communities and bars in Providence and Portland.

Bay Windows (www.baywindows. com) is a free weekly newspaper covering LGBTQ news, culture, and nightlife in Boston and New England. There's also http://outinboston.com and http:// boston.edgemedianetwork.com.

Left luggage

Security concerns in recent years have resulted in left-luggage facilities being closed in places such as bus and train stations. Your best option is to ask whether you can leave luggage at your hotel.

Lost property

Most establishments operate their own lost-and-found department, but if you lose something in a public area, go to the local police station in the event it was turned in.

Lost or stolen credit cards:
Amex: tel: 1-800-528-4800
Diners Club/Carte Blanche: tel: 1-800-234-6377
MasterCard: tel: 1-800-627-8372
Visa: tel: 1-800-847-2911

M

Maps

Insight Guides' *FlexiMap Boston* is laminated for durability and easy folding, and contains travel information as well as exceptionally clear cartography. For driving, try *The American Map New England Road Atlas* (www.american map.com).

Media

Newspapers. As well as the US nationals, such as *USA Today* and the financial *Wall Street Journal*, New England has many local newspapers, including *The Boston Globe* (www.boston.com), *Boston Herald* (www.bostonherald. com), *Hartford Courant* (www.courant. com), *Portland Press Herald* (www. pressherald.com),and *Burlington Free*

Rotunda at Boston's Quincy Market

Press (www.burlingtonfreepress.com). *The Christian Science Monitor* (www.csmonitor.com), a prestigious newspaper published in Boston on weekdays, is strong on international news, and throughout New England you will be able to get hold of copies of *The New York Times* (www.nytimes.com).

Magazines. The Improper Bostonian (www.improper.com), a free bi-weekly magazine, includes entertainment listings. A good online source is DigBoston (https://digboston.com). Out in western Massachusetts, the Valley Advocate (www.valleyadvocate.com) is a great resource for Pioneer Valley.

Useful monthly magazines include Boston Magazine (www.bostonmagazine.com), Yankee (www.yankeemagazine.com), and the Maine-focused Down East (www.downeast.com).

Television. Most hotels receive the three major national networks (ABC, CBS, and NBC), many cable networks including CNN, Fox, and ESPN (sports), and several premium movie channels, including HBO. The Public Broadcasting System (PBS) has some of the better-quality programs.

Radio. AM radio is geared toward talk, news, and information programming. FM stations tend to offer specific music formats, such as country or classic rock. Red Sox games are broadcast on over 60 stations throughout New England, anchored in Boston by WRKO-680 AM (www.wrko.com) and WEEI-93.7 FM (www.weei.com). New England Patri-

ots games are aired on WBCN-98.5 FM (www.wbcn.com). National Public Radio (www.npr.org), known for in-depth news coverage, classical music, and special programing, has affiliates throughout New England.

Money

Currency

Paper money is issued in $1, $5, $10, $20, $50, and $100 denominations.

Coins come in seven denominations: 1¢ (a penny); 5¢ (a nickel); 10¢ (a dime); 25¢ (a quarter); 50¢ (a half dollar; infrequently seen); gold-colored coins worth $1 (which are nearly the same size and hue as the quarter and are universally despised and rarely used); and the rarely-seen silver dollar.

ATMs

ATMs are ubiquitous in all but the smallest of towns throughout New England, and, although they charge a fee, they are an extremely convenient way to get cash as you need it. They will convert your transaction automatically at a generally good rate. Unlike Europe, most places in the US are not equipped to handle currency exchange, even in major cities.

Credit cards

Credit cards are almost universally accepted, except in some very small towns and a few eateries. Some are more welcome than others. Visa and MasterCard are taken almost every-

Twilight at Rowes Wharf in Boston

where, but American Express is occasionally not accepted. Discover is another card with relatively wide acceptance. Most cards charge a fee of 3 percent for international transactions and do not convert at a favorable rate. Almost all retailers accept debit card purchases and pre-paid debit cards.

Currency exchange
International visitors can exchange funds at exchange booths at Logan Airport: Sovereign Bank BCE Travelex Foreign Exchange (tel: 800-287 7362; www.travelex.com) booths are open daily at terminals B and E, and they have an office open daily at 745 Boylston Street in downtown Boston. There is a Bank of America Exchange at terminal C. All exchanges charge a processing, service, and/or administration fee,

Up-to-the-minute exchange rates are posted on www.x-rates.

Travelers' cheques
Though they are becoming less and less popular, travelers' checks are accepted by many businesses, although smaller establishments may be hesitant to accept, and make change for, larger denominations. When exchanging checks for cash, you will get the best rate at banks: hotels generally give a poor rate. Most financial establishments will charge a commission fee when cashing travelers' checks.

Tipping
Tipping is voluntary, but waiters, taxi drivers, bartenders etc will all expect a gratuity amounting to 15 percent of the bill, or 20 percent for above-average service. On restaurant checks over $100, a 20 percent tip is the norm. Tips are not included in restaurant checks, except for big parties; when calculating, do not tip on tax. Doormen, skycaps (airport porters), and porters receive about $1 per bag.

Tax
All New England states levy taxes on meals and accommodation, and all but New Hampshire on all sales. When restaurants and hotels quote prices, these taxes are not normally included – so ask, as they can bump up the cost by up to 12 percent.

Ticket prices for transport have the tax included.

Post
Post offices are usually open Mon–Fri 8am–5pm, Sat 8am–noon. In Boston, the main post office is at 25 Dorchester Street (behind South Station; tel: 617-654-5302; www.usps.gov; daily 24 hours). Mail may be addressed to General Delivery at any post office; make sure the zip code is included in the address. At time of printing, it cost $1.15 to send a postcard or a letter to Europe.

S

Smoking

The legal age in New England to buy tobacco is 18. Smoking is banned in most indoor public places and on transport. All states ban smoking in restaurants. Hotels have non-smoking rooms; many inns and B&Bs ban smoking.

T

Telephones

Phone numbers. All telephone numbers have 10 digits. If you are calling outside the local area then a 1 precedes the 10-digit number.

The Greater Boston area code, included in the number even when calling within the city, is 617. Surrounding towns use 508 (Plymouth and Provincetown), 781 (Lexington and Concord), and 978 (Salem and Cape Ann).

Four states in New England have one code each: Maine (207), New Hampshire (603), Rhode Island (401), and Vermont (802). In Connecticut, Hartford numbers are preceded by 860, those for New Haven by 203. Check all other locations in the directory.

Numbers beginning with codes 800 or 888 are toll-free if dialled within the US. **Calling from abroad.** To contact the US from the UK, dial 00 (international code) + 1 (US) + a 10-digit number. For calls to other countries from the US, dial the international access code (011), then the country code, city code, and local number. Directory assistance is 555-1212 preceded by 1 and the area code you are calling from or inquiring about; so for Boston dial 1-617-555-1212.

Cell phones. The popularity of cell phones means that you will find few public telephone booths across New England. Newer handsets from Europe and Asia work in US cities, but reception in suburban and rural areas tends to be patchy. This is improving as the US upgrades its cell infrastructure. Pay-as-you-go SIMS that will work in your phone, depending on the model, can be purchased from outlets throughout the region. Main companies are AT&T (www.att.com), Sprint (www.sprint.com), and Verizon (www.verizon.com).

Time zones

All of New England is on Eastern Standard Time: three hours ahead of Los Angeles, one hour ahead of Chicago, five hours behind London, and 15 hours behind Tokyo. New England is one hour behind the Canadian provinces of New Brunswick and Nova Scotia. Daylight Saving Time is in effect between specified dates in early April and early November; turn clocks ahead one hour in spring, back one hour in fall.

Tourist information

Connecticut Commission on Culture & Tourism, 2nd floor, 1 Constitution Plaza, Hartford; tel: 860-256-280/1-888-288-4748; www.ctvisit.com.

Coming in to land at Logan Airport

Maine Office of Tourism, 59 State House Station, Augusta; tel: 1-888-624-6345; www.visitmaine.com.

Massachusetts Office of Travel and Tourism, 10 Park Plaza, Suite 4510, Boston; tel: 617-973-8500/1-800-227-6277; www.massvacation.com.

New Hampshire Office of Travel & Tourism Development, 172 Pembroke Road, Concord; tel: 603-271-2665/1-800-386-4664; www.visitnh.gov.

Rhode Island Tourism Division, 315 Iron Horse Way, Providence; tel: 1-800-556-2484; www.visitrhodeisland.com.

Vermont Department of Tourism & Marketing, 1 National Life Drive, 6th floor, Montpelier; tel: 802-828-3237/1-800-837-6668; www.vermontvacation.com.

Boston and Cambridge

The **Greater Boston Convention & Visitors Bureau** (2 Copley Place; tel: 617-536-4100/1-888-733-2678; www.bostonusa.com) runs two visitor centers:

Boston Common Visitor Information Center, 148 Tremont Street; Mon–Fri 8.30am–5pm, Sat–Sun 9am–5pm (the booth here marks the start of the Freedom Trail).

Prudential Visitor Center, Center Court, Prudential Center, 800 Boylston Street; Mon–Sat 10am–5pm, Sun 11am–8pm.

The **Cambridge Office of Tourism** (4 Brattle Street; tel: 617-441-2884/1-800-862-5678; www.cambridgeusa. org;) has a booth in the center of Harvard Square (tel: 617-497-1630; Mon–Fri 9am–5pm, Sat–Sun 9am–1pm).

Transportation

Arrival by air

Boston's **Logan Airport** (tel: 1-800-235-6426, www.massport.com), the main access point for international travelers to New England, has four terminals (A, B, C, E). Airlines do not necessarily use the same terminal for domestic and international flights. There are free wheelchair-lift-equipped shuttle buses that run between the terminals.

Regional airports include:

Bradley International, Windsor Locks, Connecticut; tel: 860-292-2000; www.bradleyairport.com.

Portland International Jetport, Portland, Maine; tel: 207-774-7301; www.portlandjetport.org.

Manchester-Boston Regional Airport, 1 Airport Road, Manchester, New Hampshire; tel: 603-624-6556; www.flymanchester.com.

T. F. Green Airport, 2000 Post Road, Warwick, Rhode Island; tel: 401-737-8222; www.pvdairport.com.

Burlington International Airport, Airport Drive, South Burlington, Vermont; tel: 802-863-2874; www.btv.aero.

Each state also has several smaller airports, most with limited commuter service. Visitors to southern parts of New England often choose to fly into one of the major New York City area airports – Kennedy, La Guardia, or Newark

Mountain biking at Killington

– and continue their travels via rail, bus, or rental car.

Arrival by land

By train. Amtrak (tel: 1-800-872-7245; www.amtrak.com) operates several routes that serve major New England cities and points in between. Boston's South Station is the north terminus of Amtrak's Northeast Corridor, linking the city with New York and Washington, DC, via Providence and New Haven; trains – including the high-speed, extra-fare Acela – run frequently every day. The Lake Shore Limited runs daily between Boston and Chicago, with stops at Worcester and Springfield, Massachusetts. The Downeaster connects Boston's North Station with Portland, Maine. The Vermonter operates daily between Washington, DC, and St Albans, Vermont, via New York City, Hartford, Springfield, and major Vermont cities and towns. The Ethan Allen Express runs between New York and Rutland, Vermont.

By bus. Greyhound (tel: 1-800-231-2222; www.greyhound.com) and its regional affiliates serve major population centers and in-between points throughout New England, and link the region with its terminals in New York, Montreal, and points south and west.

By car. New England is well served by the US Interstate Highway system. I-95, the coastal artery, connects New York with New Haven, Providence, Boston, and Portland. East–west I-84 links southern New York State with eastern Massachusetts via Hartford. The Massachusetts Turnpike (I-90) joins the New York Thruway near Albany. North–south I-89 crosses into Vermont from Quebec southeast of Montreal, and links with Boston-bound I-93 at Concord, New Hampshire. North–south I-91 runs between New Haven and the Vermont-Quebec border.

Within New England

Driving. New England is best traveled by automobile. In addition to the Interstate Highway system, the region is served by an excellent system of secondary federal and state highways, and county and municipal roads. Roads are generally well maintained, with every effort made to remove snow promptly; but in rural areas you might encounter miles of unpaved roads that can be tricky in winter or in the mud season that arrives with the spring thaw.

Road signs can cause problems even for experienced locals – you won't have trouble on major routes, but you may feel abandoned on some secondary roads. It is always a good idea to travel with detailed maps or GPS.

The speed limit on Interstate Highways in New England is 65mph (105kph), except in urban areas where it is 55mph (90kph). On secondary highways in rural areas it is usually 50mph (80kph). In built-up areas you must

Boston ferries

slow to 20–40mph (32–64kph); city speed limits rarely exceed 25mph (40 kph). Look out for signs – limits can change abruptly, especially on the outskirts of towns. A right turn on a red traffic signal is permissible after a complete stop anywhere in New England, except where there is a No Turn on Red sign. At a rotary (roundabout), yield to vehicles already in it.

Car rental. Major US car-rental firms are represented at Boston's Logan Airport, as well as at smaller airports and city locations throughout New England. Note that drivers must be 21 to rent a car, and that rental agreements may forbid taking a car rented in New England to New York or New Jersey without payment of a surcharge. Children under the age of five or under 40lbs (18kg) must be protected by a child safety seat, available at extra cost.

By train. In addition to Amtrak routes, commuter rail transportation is provided in eastern Massachusetts and between Boston and Providence by the Massachusetts Bay Transportation Authority (tel: 617-222-3200/1-800-392-6100; www.mbta.com). The MBTA also operates Boston's system of subways (called 'the T'), trolleys, and elevated trains.

To use the subway, purchase a CharlieTicket ($2.75) from the machines in the stations. A single ticket permits travel on the entire 'Outbound' length of a line, but there's an 'Inbound' surcharge on extensions of the Green Line. If you board the T at surface stations where there is no ticket machine, you will need the exact fare as conductors do not carry change.

The CharlieCard is a plastic stored-value card. If you use this, then each ride is $2.25 and you can get free transfers to MBTA buses (not possible with the CharlieTickets). Accompanied children under 11 travel free.

By bus. An MBTA bus service connects Boston with its suburbs and outlying cities. Other city areas in New England also have a local bus service. For inter-city bus travel within the region, contact Greyhound (see opposite) or Peter Pan Bus Lines (tel: 1-800-343-9999; www.peterpanbus.com). Plymouth and Brockton Buses (tel: 508-746-0378; www.p-b.com) link Boston with Cape Cod and Massachusetts's South Shore, while C&J (tel: 603-430-1100; www.ridecj.com) offers a bus service between Boston and Portsmouth.

By ferry. Between mid-May and October it is possible to catch ferries from Boston to Salem and to Provincetown (www.bostonharborcruises.com and www.baystatecruisecompany.com).

Taxis

Portland, Maine: ASAP Taxi, tel: 207-791-2727, www.asaptaxi.net.

Boston, Massachusetts: Boston Cab, tel: 617-536-5010; The Good Taxi tel: 617-855-6500.

Cambridge, Massachusetts: Cambridge Taxi Cab, tel: 617-649-7000; Green Cab & Yellow Cab, tel: 617-876-5000.

Riding the T

Portsmouth, New Hampshire: Great Bay Taxi, tel: 603-431-4555, www.greatbaytaxi.com.

Providence, Rhode Island: Airport Taxis, tel: 401-737-2868, www.airporttaxiri.com.

Burlington, Vermont: Green Cab, tel: 802-864-2424, http://greencabvt.com.

Passes

Boston LinkPass. The LinkPass is a cost-effective way for visitors to use the MBTA system in and around Boston. It allows unlimited use of the subway, buses, water shuttle, and Zone 1A of the commuter rail lines for one ($12) or seven days ($21.25), or one month ($84.50). LinkPass cards can be purchased at almost all stations. Monthly LinkPasses are only valid on subways and buses.

City Tourist Card. The Boston Card (tel: 1-800-887-9103; www.smartdestinations.com) is a one-, two-, three-, five-, or seven-day visitor pass, which offers unlimited admission to more than 41 attractions and tours in and around Boston. Cards can be bought online and downloaded to any mobile device or printed at home

Visas and passports

Immigration and visitation procedures can change rapidly depending on real and perceived threats to security.

To enter the United States, foreign visitors need a passport and many also need a visa. You may be asked to provide evidence that you intend to leave the United States after your visit is over (usually in the form of a return or onward ticket).

You may not need a visa if you are a resident of one of 27 countries that participate in the Visa Waiver Program (VWP) and are planning to stay in the US for less than 90 days. Consult the nearest US embassy or consulate in your home country or check www.travel.state.gov. You must, however, log onto the Electronic System for Travel Authorization's unmemorably named website, www.cbp.gov/travel/international-visitors/esta at least 48 hours before traveling and provide personal information and travel details; either your application will be accepted (and will be valid for multiple visits over two years) or you will be told to apply for a visa.

Websites

For general tourist information about New England, see www.visitnewengland.com and www.discovernewengland.org.

BOOKS AND FILM

New England lends itself to poetry. The ocean waves crash against its rocky shore; snow caps its mountains, mists settle in the valleys, and the thick forests explode with reds, yellows, and oranges in the fall. It has provided no shortage of material to America's first generations of writers, like Nathaniel Hawthorne, Henry David Thoreau, and Louisa May Alcott, and kept artistic exploration well-watered at intellectual institutions like Harvard, Yale, Dartmouth, and Brown, albeit with an eye to morality.

The lush, timeless beauty also found visual expression, first in paintings, and later in mass-produced Currier & Ives lithograph prints. It was Norman Rockwell, however, that made the New England image a spiritual American icon. Filmmakers took full advantage of the natural and historical backdrop as well, from the 1908 adaptation of *The Scarlet Letter* to the Oscar winning *Manchester by the Sea* in 2016. Boston, as the major city of New England and one of the country's most historically significant, plays a particularly leading role in every genre, be it crime in *The Departed*, romance in *Love Story*, comedy in *Legally Blonde*, or technology in *The Social Network*. The richness of New England provides ample fodder for all.

Books

History and culture

Builders of the Bay Colony, by Samuel Eliot Morison. New England's most celebrated historian tells the story of the men – and one woman – who gave New England its intellectual underpinnings.

A Week on the Concord and Merrimack Rivers, Walden, The Maine Woods, and Cape Cod, by Henry David Thoreau. Thoreau's four greatest works describe his travels on foot and by canoe – and his sojourn at Walden Pond; detailed descriptions of mid-19th-century landscape and people combine with the blunt, often ornery musings of an archetypal New England intellect.

Paul Revere's Ride, by David Hackett Fischer. Historian Fischer explains what really happened on that April night, which is a lot juicier and more interesting than what's generally taught in school.

The Encyclopedia of New England, edited by Burt Feintuch and David H. Watters. A magisterial compendium of New England persons, places, and accomplishments (in the same vein, look for New England University Press's **The Vermont Encyclopedia**, edited by Duffy, Hand, and Orth. A very readable Green Mountain gather-all.

The Proper Bostonians, by Cleveland Amory. Not satire or skewering, but a

Iconic scenes in 'Jaws'

lighthearted yet near-anthropological study of a Brahmin elite with 'grandfather on the brain.'

The Prince of Providence, by Mike Stanton. The story of very colorful Providence mayor Buddy Cianci, who oversaw the rebirth of his city and was convicted of corruption while still in office.

The Enduring Shore: A History of Cape Cod, Martha's Vineyard, and Nantucket, by Paul Schneider. Natural and social history, with an emphasis on human impact on a fragile, ultimately ephemeral environment.

The Outermost House: A Year of Life on the Great Beach of Cape Cod, by Henry Beston. Beston's classic rivals Thoreau's Walden as an account of a year of blissful solitude in the loveliest of natural surroundings.

String Too Short to Be Saved: Recollections of Summers on a New England Farm, by Donald Hall. A poet's warm, elegiac recollections of life on his grandfather's small New England farm in the 1940s.

The Survival of the Bark Canoe, by John McPhee. An account of a Maine river trip in a modern bark canoe, interwoven with the story of an uncompromising New Englander who builds the timeless craft.

The Lobster Chronicles: Life on a Very Small Island, by Linda Greenlaw. New England's iconic fishery, seen from the inside by one of the first women captains to break a famously rigid gender barrier.

All Souls, by Michael Patrick MacDonald. A searing memoir of an anguished childhood growing up in Boston's Irish housing projects.

Mayflower, by Nathaniel Philbrick. A well-researched, entertainingly written, unvarnished, and unromantic account of the Pilgrims.

A Civil Action, by Jonathan Harr. Story of Woburn MA and its suits against two large firms held responsible for polluting the town's water source and causing illness and death.

Hackers, by Steven Levy. Largely focusing on MIT, it explores how hackers are responsible for the increasing sophistication of computer technology.

Landscape and natural history

A Guide to New England's Landscape, by Neil Jorgensen. Written in layperson's English, a comprehensive look at how today's mountains, lakes, farmland, and coastline evolved in deep and recent geologic time.

Hands on the Land: A History of the Vermont Landscape, by Jan Albers. The story of human interaction with the land the glaciers left – a never-easy process that yielded a remarkably beautiful balance between the natural and built environments.

In Season: A Natural History of the New England Year, by Nona Bell Estrin. In a region with some of the world's sharpest seasonal divisions, the drama of life's winter ebb and summer flow.

Cod, by Mark Kurlansky. A surprisingly

fascinating account of how codfish and the fishing industry impacted New England and the rest of the world.

The Secret Life of Lobsters, by Trevor Corson. Told from the perspectives of lobstermen and marine biologists, it explores the near-collapse of the lobster industry in the 1980s and unravels the mysteries of a lobster's life cycle, living arrangements, and mating habits, often in hysterical detail.

Not Without Peril, by Nicholas Howe. Stories of climbers in New Hampshire's Presidential range from 1849 to 1994.

Architecture

Houses of Boston's Back Bay: An Architectural History, 1840–1917, by Bainbridge Bunting. A social as well as an architectural history, this amply illustrated book describes the evolution – and living style – of Boston's fist planned neighborhood.

New England's Architecture, by Wallace Nutting. A fine collection of sketches and photographs drawn from books on the architecture of individual New England states by the late antiquarian Nutting, who pioneered the preservation of the region's vintage homes and furnishings.

Spenser's Boston, by Robert Parker. A photographic journey in and around the city with the author of the popular mystery series as your guide. Quite a few settings from the novels, of course, but it's really a love letter from Parker to his city.

Fiction

Writing New England: An Anthology from the Puritans to the Present, edited by Andrew Delbanco. This carefully chosen collection of New England authors represents nearly four centuries of the region's intellectual development.

The Late George Apley, by John P. Marquand. A deft and wry portrayal of a Brahmin trapped within his class, as its grip on Boston weakens.

The Last Hurrah, by Edwin O'Connor. The ethnic-based machine politics of 20th-century Boston shape the career of a protagonist based on Boston's roguish Mayor James Michael Curley.

Northern Borders, by Howard Frank Mosher. A coming-of-age tale, set among Mosher's vanishing breed of back-country Vermonters equally at home with sawmills and Shakespeare.

Empire Falls, by Richard Russo. The Pulitzer Prize-winning novel of a mill town's deterioration.

Blues, by John Hersey. An old fisherman and a youth explore Cape Cod, life, and the New England outdoors.

An Arsonist's Guide to Writers' Homes in New England, by Brock Clarke. A wonderful send-up of memoirs, mystery fiction, and the adulation of New England's literary icons.

Films

Manchester by the Sea (2016). This tale of a man who looks after his teenage nephew after his brother dies won

Oscar–winning Casey Affleck in 'Manchester by the Sea'

two Oscars, including best actor for Massachusetts' own Casey Affleck.

Ted (2012). Comedy starring Mark Wahlberg as a Boston native whose childhood teddy bear, Ted, suddenly comes alive.

The Ghost Writer (2010). Starring Ewan McGregor and Pierce Brosnan, and directed by Roman Polanski, this is a political thriller adapted from Robert Harris' novel set in a fictional Massachusetts village.

Revolutionary Road (2008). Based on the Richard Yates novel, this classy drama depicts the disaffections of striving Connecticut suburbanites in the 1950s.

The Departed (2006). Martin Scorsese's Oscar-winning take on the Boston underworld. Jack Nicholson's character was allegedly based on fugitive gangster Whitey Bulger.

Little Children (2006). Kate Winslet stars as the matriarch of a family surviving a tumultuous summer in a Boston suburb.

Mystic River (2003). Director Clint Eastwood's retelling of the Dennis Lehane novel, examining lives tightly intertwined in a working-class Irish Boston neighborhood.

The Perfect Storm (2000). Starring George Clooney and based on the real-life *Andrea Gail* tragedy, this is a paean to the 10,000 Gloucester men who have lost their lives in the North Atlantic fishery.

Dead Poets Society (1989). This classic, set in a New England prep school,
centers on Robin Williams's performance as an inspiring English teacher.

Beetlejuice (1988). Set in Connecticut, but filmed in Vermont, this cult classic sees Alec Baldwin, Geena Davis, and Michael Keaton as ghosts trying to scare away New Yorkers.

The Bostonians (1984). An elegant Merchant-Ivory production brings to the screen Henry James's tale of propriety's clash with social activism in the 19th-century Hub.

On Golden Pond (1981). Filmed at New Hampshire's Squam Lake, this was Henry Fonda's final role, as crusty Yankee professor Norman Thayer.

Jaws (1975). The film that kept thousands out of the water and inspired many nightmares brings a hungry great white shark to fictional Amity Island, really Martha's Vineyard in Massachusetts

Love Story (1970). 'Love means never having to say you're sorry' claimed this blockbuster romantic drama starring Ali MacGraw and Ryan O'Neal

The Thomas Crown Affair (1968). Steve McQueen robs for pleasure while under pursuit by private investigator Faye Dunaway, as seduction sparks fly.

The Last Hurrah (1958). A political drama based on the career of Boston Mayor James M. Curley, featuring Spencer Tracy as a master of machine politics.

Northwest Passage (1940). Features Spencer Tracy as French-and-Indian War hero Major Robert Rogers, in one of cinema's better New England historical dramas; they even got the geography right.

ABOUT THIS BOOK

This *Explore Guide* has been produced by the editors of Insight Guides, whose books have set the standard for visual travel guides since 1970. With top-quality photography and authoritative recommendations, these guidebooks bring you the very best routes and itineraries in the world's most exciting destinations.

BEST ROUTES

The routes in the book provide something to suit all budgets, tastes and trip lengths. As well as covering the destination's many classic attractions, the itineraries track lesser-known sights. The routes embrace a range of interests, so whether you are an art fan, a gourmet, a history buff or have kids to entertain, you will find an option to suit.

We recommend reading the whole of a route before setting out. This should help you to familiarise yourself with it and enable you to plan where to stop for refreshments – options are shown in the 'Food and Drink' box at the end of each tour.

For our pick of the tours by theme, consult Recommended Routes for... (see pages 6–7).

INTRODUCTION

The routes are set in context by this introductory section, giving an overview of the destination to set the scene, plus background information on food and drink, shopping and more, while a succinct history timeline highlights the key events over the centuries.

DIRECTORY

Also supporting the routes is a Directory chapter, with a clearly organised A–Z of practical information, our pick of where to stay while you are there and select restaurant listings; these eateries complement the more low-key cafés and restaurants that feature within the routes and are intended to offer a wider choice for evening dining. Also included here are some nightlife listings and our recommendations for books and films about the destination.

ABOUT THE AUTHORS

Raised in Burlington, Vermont and educated in Boston, Massachusetts, Mike Dunphy has written extensively about New England for travel guides. His resume also includes features for CNN, *USA Today*, *Travel Weekly*, *Huffington Post*, *DuJour*, *Tablet*, *Metro*, and *Beer Advocate*, among many others.

This book builds on original content by Simon Richmond, and Bill and Kay Scheller.

CONTACT THE EDITORS

We hope you find this Explore Guide useful, interesting and a pleasure to read. If you have any questions or feedback on the text, pictures or maps, please do let us know. If you have noticed any errors or outdated facts, or have suggestions for places to include on the routes, we would be delighted to hear from you. Please drop us an email at hello@insightguides.com. Thanks!

CREDITS

Explore New England
Editor: Sarah Clark
Author: Mike Dunphy
Head of Production: Rebeka Davies
Update Production: Apa Digital
Picture Editor: Tom Smyth
Cartography: original cartography
Berndtson & Berndtson, updated by Carte
Photo credits: Allium Restaurant 110; AWL
Images 4/5T, 8/9T, 28/29T; Billings Farm
76; Boston Symphony Orchestra 24; Café
This Way 117; Castle in the Clouds 83;
Claire Folger/Kobal/REX/Shutterstock 137;
Discover New England 4MC, 6TL, 8MC,
12/13, 28MR, 57L, 60, 63L, 76/77, 81L,
96MR; Felt 96MC; Fotolia 7M, 74, 74/75;
Frank Mullin 66/67; Getty Images 116,
118; iStock 1, 4MC, 10, 11, 12, 14/15, 27,
66, 67L, 70/71, 75L, 78, 78/79, 80, 82,
88, 90, 94; Killington and American Skiing
Co 131; Kindra Clineff 4MR, 4ML, 6ML,
8ML, 8ML, 8MR, 13L, 17, 18, 20, 23L,
22/23, 25, 28ML, 28ML, 28MR, 58/59,
61L, 60/61, 62, 62/63, 64, 65, 70, 71L,
72, 73, 79L, 80/81, 84, 89L, 88/89, 92,
93L, 92/93L, 95, 120, 124, 125; Leonardo
77L, 99, 100, 102, 103, 104, 105; Massachusetts Office of Travel & Tourism 56;
Mount Washington Cog Railway 86/87;
Mount Washington Resort 85; Moviestore/
REX/Shutterstock 134, 136; Newport,
RI Convention & Visitors Bureau 68, 69;
Nowitz Photography/Apa Publications 4ML,
4MR, 6MC, 7T, 7MR, 7MR, 8MC, 8MR,
16B, 16T, 19L, 18/19, 21L, 20/21, 22, 26,
28MC, 30, 31, 32, 33, 34, 35L, 34/35, 36,
37, 38, 39, 40, 41, 42, 43L, 42/43, 44, 45,
46, 47, 48, 49L, 48/49, 50, 51, 52, 53, 54,
55, 56/57, 58, 59L, 96ML, 96MC, 96MR,
96/97T, 98, 111, 119, 122, 123, 126, 127,
128, 129, 130, 132, 133; Portland Museum of Art 28MC, 91; Shakespeare & Company 96ML, 121; Shutterstock 106/107,
112; The Brass Key 101; The Chanler 113;
The Simon Pearce Restaurant 114, 115;
Top of the Hub 108, 109; Universal/Kobal/
REX/Shutterstock 134/135
Cover credits: Shutterstock (main&bottom)

Printed by CTPS – China

DISTRIBUTION

UK, Ireland and Europe
Apa Publications (UK) Ltd
sales@insightguides.com
United States and Canada
Ingram Publisher Services
ips@ingramcontent.com
Australia and New Zealand
Woodslane
info@woodslane.com.au
Southeast Asia
Apa Publications (Singapore) Pte
singaporeoffice@insightguides.com
Hong Kong, Taiwan and China
Apa Publications (HK) Ltd
hongkongoffice@insightguides.com
Worldwide
Apa Publications (UK) Ltd
sales@insightguides.com

SPECIAL SALES, CONTENT LICENSING AND COPUBLISHING

Insight Guides can be purchased in bulk
quantities at discounted prices. We can
create special editions, personalised jackets
and corporate imprints tailored to your needs.
sales@insightguides.com
www.insightguides.biz

INDEX

MAP LEGEND

- Start of tour
- Tour & route direction
- ❶ Recommended sight
- ❷ Recommended restaurant/café
- ★ Place of interest
- ❶ Tourist information
- ✈ Airport
- Railway
- Motorway
- Main bus station

- -·-- Ferry route
- ✉ Main post office
- ✚ Cathedral or church
- ✡ Synagogue
- 𝟏 Statue/monument
- 𝐌̂ Museum/gallery
- Theatre
- 𝓵 Lighthouse
- ⌐ Beach
- ⛷ Ski resort
- ☼ Viewpoint

- ♎ Cave
- Important building
- Urban area
- Hotel
- Pedestrian area
- Shop / mall
- Park
- Non-urban area
- National park / state park
- -·-- State boundary